# A GUIDE TO PSALMS

## TEF Study Guides

This SPCK series was originally sponsored and subsidized by the Theological Education Fund of the WCC in response to requests from Africa, Asia, the Caribbean, and the Pacific. The books are prepared by and in consultation with theological tutors from all over the world, but have from the outset been as widely used by students and parish groups in the West as by those for whom English may be a second language. More advanced titles in the list are marked (A).

*General Editors*: Daphne Terry and Nicholas Beddow

### IN PREPARATION

TEF Study Guide 6

# A GUIDE TO PSALMS

John Hargreaves

First published 1973
SPCK
Holy Trinity Church
Marylebone Road, London NW1 4DU

Eighth impression 1991 (with amendments)

The photographs in this book are reproduced by
courtesy of Eric Anderson and Jonathan
Hargreaves (on p. 108), USPG (on p. 4), and
Camera Press Ltd.

ISBN 0 281 02590 8 (net)
ISBN 0 281 02695 5 (non-net edition for Africa,
Asia, S. Pacific, and Caribbean)

Made and printed in Great Britain by
Hollen Street Press Ltd, Slough, Berks

# Contents

# Preface

No one ever disliked the Psalms more than I did for the first thirty years of my life! They seemed impossible to understand. Many of them were so un-Christian. People sang them so mournfully. Or so it seemed to me. Then I joined the staff of a theological college and to my dismay was asked to conduct a course on the Psalms. But my dismay did not last. Before very long I had discovered, and I believe some of the students had discovered, how precious the Psalms are. To our surprise we found not only that they were great songs and poems of faith in God, but that they had been written out of experiences and in situations such as we ourselves knew well. And we had tremendous joy in singing them, sometimes to music which the students had composed.

So I have tried in this book to pass on what we discovered. I hope it will be found useful, whether the reader is accustomed to singing the Psalms or not. If it is useful, this will be due to the many other people who have since given me help: to the Reverend Professor Peter Ackroyd of King's College, London; Canon Dennis Gooderson, now of St Michael's, Cumnor; Father Jonathan Graham, then Superior of the Community of the Resurrection, Mirfield; the Reverend John Lamb, then Librarian of New College, Edinburgh; the Reverend Basil Minchin of the Fellowship of St Alban and St Sergius; the Reverend Cyril Rodd, of Southlands College, Wimbledon; Miss Greta Preston of the Church Missionary Society; the Reverend Juergen Simonson, now of St Margaret's, Putney; and the Reverend Philip Turner, then of Bishop Tucker College in Uganda; to members of St Luke's Church, Sevenoaks; the staff of the CMS Fellowship House in Chislehurst; St Julian's Community in Sussex; and to Miss Daphne Terry and Mrs Joyce Chapman, who as Editor and Secretary respectively of the Theological Education Fund's English Textbook Programme, have taken immense care over the book at every stage, and, in addition, given me great help of all kinds.

*Sevenoaks,* 1972                                        JOHN HARGREAVES

# Using this Guide

Twenty psalms only have been chosen for special consideration in this Guide, in order that readers may study each one in detail. They are the twenty psalms which, as far as the author can discover, are those which Christians are using more than others today.

But reference is made to many other psalms, together with notes. And readers will find that they can study other psalms by the same method which is used in each chapter of this Guide.

*The first chapter* shows that *the Psalms are for all generations.* It takes the place of an Introduction, and should be read first so that fullest use may be made of the other chapters.

*The arrangement* of each subsequent chapter is as follows:

First, a study of the *experience* from which the writer wrote his psalm. Readers will find that they have had similar experiences themselves.

Secondly, a study of the ways in which the writer *recognized God* in the experience, and of what people at that time believed about Him. We use the Psalms today only because the writers (and worshippers) went beyond their experiences and turned towards God Himself, the same Lord whom we worship today.

Thirdly, a study of the psalm itself, which was the *response* which the writer and worshippers made to God.

Lastly, notes on particular verses and subjects which seem to need further explanation or discussion.

The full text of the twenty psalms has not been included in this Guide. This means that *it is necessary to read each psalm carefully, in the Bible,* before reading the chapter about it, and at each stage of the study.

*Three General Notes* are included: *The Psalms were for Temple worship* (p. 44), to which a study of Psalm 24 is attached; *The Psalms are for singing* (p. 116), to which a study of Psalm 98 is attached, and *The Psalms were written and collected over many years* (p. 174). These General Notes provide information which refers to *all* psalms, and some people may prefer to read them, after they have read the first chapter, before going on to the detailed work on particular psalms.

*A list of subjects and occasions* for which people often use psalms in worship will be found on p. 177, together with the particular psalms most often found suitable for each. This list may be useful to those who plan public services, as well as to others who use the Psalms privately.

*Study suggestions* appear at the end of each chapter and each General Note. They are intended to help readers who are working alone to study more thoroughly and understand the Psalms more clearly, and to check their own progress. They can also be used in the classroom, and provide topics for group research and discussion. They relate to:

1. *Words:* These are to help readers to check and deepen their understanding of some important words and phrases.
2. *Content:* These questions will help a reader to check his own work and ensure he has fully grasped the ideas and points of teaching studied.
3. *Bible:* These provide an opportunity to compare the ideas and teaching in the Psalms with ideas and teaching found in other parts of the Bible.
4. *Discussion and research:* These suggestions will help readers to think out and discuss (a) the practical application of the truths and teaching in the Psalms to everyday life, and (b) ways in which Christians today can use psalms in their public and private worship.

The best way to use these Study Suggestions is: first, re-read the psalm itself; secondly, read the appropriate section of the Guide carefully once or twice; and lastly, do the work suggested, in writing or group discussion, without looking at the Guide again except when there is an instruction to do so.

*The Key* at the end of the book (p. 178) will enable readers to check their work on those questions which can be checked in this way. In most cases the Key does not give the answer to questions; it shows where an answer is to be found, either in the Guide or in the Bible.

*Please note* that all these study suggestions are only *suggestions*. Some readers may not want to use them at all. Some teachers may want to select only those which are relevant to a particular situation, or may prefer to substitute questions of their own.

*The Index* (p. 183) includes only the more important proper names of people and places and the main subjects which occur in the psalms studied or which are discussed in the Guide.

*Bible Version:* The English translation of the Bible used in the Guide is the *Revised Standard Version of the Bible* (RSV). The *New English Bible* (NEB) is used in a few cases where it shows the meaning more clearly.

*The Bibliography* on p. 176 lists some books about the Psalms which readers may find useful for further study.

# Introduction
## The Psalms are for all generations
## Example, Psalm 118

A good way to discover what sort of writings the Psalms are is to look at one psalm in particular. We have chosen here Psalm 118, and we shall consider six examples of how it has been used at different times in history. The first example is of the days when the Israelites had just returned to Jerusalem from Babylon. Then we shall see how it was used by Jesus and His disciples, then by Christians of AD 100, then by some monks of AD 360, then by a boy living in AD 1737, and lastly by a Christian congregation today.

### JERUSALEM, 5TH CENTURY BC

The Israelites had at last returned to Jerusalem after their long exile in Babylon; they had finished rebuilding the Temple and the city walls. Now their leaders had called them together to praise God at the autumn Feast of Tabernacles at Jerusalem. Since they had all experienced relief from the suffering of exile, their leaders had prepared a psalm of praise to God. Not all of it was a new psalm even then: it was probably based on the prayer of an Israelite leader who, long before, had had the same experience.

It is the last and great day of the feast. The priests stand in their bright robes outside the gate of the Temple courtyard; the choir is there, and the musicians with their harps and trumpets and cymbals. There is a very great crowd of rejoicing people. As they march towards the Temple, a choir begins to sing "Give thanks to the Lord for He is good", and another choir (or perhaps all the people together) shout a response "His steadfast love endures for ever" (v. 1).

As verses like v. 13 are sung: "I was pushed hard, so that I was falling, but the Lord helped me", perhaps the worshippers remember how their enemies had tried to prevent them from rebuilding the walls, and they shout the response again, "His steadfast love . . .".

At verse 19 they have reached the great door of the Temple. The priests alone sing verse 20 in the name of God, "This is the gate of the Lord" and verse 26 "Blessed be he who enters in the name of the Lord." Then the whole congregation, carrying branches of trees, go through the door: they march or dance round the altar on which an animal will later be sacrificed to God: "Bind the festal procession with branches up to the horns of the altar" (v. 27b). The psalm ends with the same great shout, "His steadfast love endures for ever."

1

## JERUSALEM, AD 20

It is evening in the upper room, and a lamp is burning. Jesus has shared with His disciples the Supper which He planned to have with them. He has given them bread and wine, showing them that He is now about to give Himself for all mankind by His death. Judas has gone out, and Jesus and the eleven disciples sing together the Psalms of Praise or "Hallel Psalms" which were used at Passover time (Mark 14.26). They have come to the last of these psalms, Psalm 118. So Jesus sings with special meaning verses such as these: "The Lord is on my side, I do not fear" (v. 6); "I shall look in triumph on those who hate me" (v. 7); "the stone which the builders rejected has become the chief corner-stone" (v. 22); "Blessed is he who enters in the name of the Lord" (v. 26); and lastly, perhaps repeated many times, the chorus verse "His steadfast love endures . . ."

Then they go outside, to the dark garden of Gethsemane.

## ROME, AD 100

A group of Christians are meeting for the "Breaking of Bread" or "Holy Communion". They are meeting secretly, at the house of one of the members, because Christians are in danger of being arrested and accused of plotting against the Emperor. But it is Easter Day, and they are praising God in the words of Psalm 118. While a boy keeps watch at the door, one of them begins, "O give thanks to the Lord, for He is good", and the little groups answer, "His steadfast love endures for ever". There are old people there, and children, who can join in with the others by singing this chorus together.

Like Jesus, the leader reaches verse 6: "The Lord is on my side, I do not fear", and the Christian worshippers are encouraged as they sing together in response: "His steadfast love . . ." They hear the words of verse 22, "The stone which the builders rejected has become the chief corner-stone", and they say to themselves, "Yes, Jesus was rejected, and now He is the Risen King". They hear verse 26 "Blessed is he who enters in the name of the Lord", and they realize that Christ is indeed present with them.

## ASIA MINOR, AD 360

It is a cold morning. Basil "the Great" and his monks have met in their chapel on the banks of the River Iris, in Cappadocia, part of the country now known as Turkey. It is still dark as they come in. Half the monks are standing on one side of the chapel, half on the other. They begin in the way that they begin every morning, with Psalm 118, and they share the singing of it. Those on one side sing the first half of each verse, those on the other side sing the second half. We can see why they chose 118 for their morning psalm when we hear them singing verse 24:

2

"This is the day the Lord has made", with the answer "Let us rejoice and be glad in it."

## ENGLAND, AD 1737

It is a school-room in England, and a boy aged six is crying bitterly. His mother has died, and his father, not knowing how to look after him, has sent him to this school, far from home. The boy suffers from sore eyes and is miserable. He is frightened, too, because he knows that a boy of fifteen will soon come and beat and kick him. "I beat you because you cry," the bigger boy says. So the small boy shares his misery and his fear with God, as he says over and over again a part of Psalm 118 which his mother had taught him, "Out of my distress I called on the Lord . . . The Lord is on my side, I do not fear."

This boy was William Cowper, who afterwards wrote the hymn "O for a closer walk with God."

## NIGERIA, TODAY

It is Easter Day and there is a great crowd of worshippers in St Stephen's Cathedral Church at Ondo in Nigeria. They have put up green palm-leaf shelters outside to protect from the hot sun those who cannot find a place inside. Everyone is in festival dress of blue and many other colours. There is a choir of fifty singers in red or blue gowns and white surplices.

The leader has just announced Psalm 118. Then Yoruba music is played and the choir sing the Chorus verse in Yoruba, to music which the organist composed: "It is better to trust in the Lord than to trust in princes" (v. 9). The psalm is then read, the leader reading one verse, the people reading the next. After some verses, there comes music from the organ again and the chorus is repeated. This time many of the people can join in. By the time that the psalm comes to an end, they all know the chorus and they all sing it, whether they are in the church or on the grass outside. They will still be singing it as they go home after the service.

So this congregation lifts its praise to God, in Yoruba words and music; and yet the people are joining themselves with worshippers in all lands and of all generations.

These examples show us what sort of writings the Psalms are:

1. The Psalms arose from people's *ordinary experience*.

The Psalms exist because Israelites, like ourselves, experienced such feelings as relief (as we see in Psalm 118) and sadness and guilt and achievement. Then in faith they recognized that God was at work behind their experience. Then they made their response to God, and their response is the psalm.

Because we today experience what Israelites experienced long ago

3

"The Psalms are for all generations" (p. 1)—and for all times and all places—
South Africa, Japan, Czechoslovakia, England . . .

(because we too see God at work), we too can use the Psalms as our response to Him.

2. They are *Israelite songs*.

All the Psalms were written by Israelites before the coming of Christ. They are prayers to God who had made a "covenant" or special agreement with the Israelites as His chosen people. See General Note C, p. 174.

3. They were part of the worship offered to God *in the Temple* at Jerusalem.

The Book of Psalms has been called the "Hymnbook and Prayerbook" of these Temple services. See General Note A, p. 44.

Many psalms were at first the prayers of individuals, which afterwards were used in public worship. Those who led this worship made changes in the psalm to fit it for public use.

But not all the Psalms were used in the Temple services. Psalm 119 was never used in this way.

4. They were *Jesus's hymns and prayers*.

This is probably the chief reason why Christians still use them. See note on p. 32 on the way that Jesus used the Psalms.

5. They have been *used by Christians* ever since Jesus used them.

"You sing psalms and hymns and spiritual songs, with thankfulness in your hearts, to God" (Col. 3.16). "Paul and Silas were singing hymns (i.e. psalms of praise) to God" (Acts 16.25).

But Christians have had to interpret the Psalms in their own way. This has not been easy, because they were written before Christ's coming.

6. They are *songs*, and Israelite musicians often accompanied them on various instruments. See General Note B, p. 116.

7. They are *prayers*, of response to God, such as:

Prayers of praise (e.g. Pss. 8, 98, 103)

Prayers for help in distress (e.g. Pss. 22, 42)

Prayers of trusting in God (e.g. Pss. 23, 91)

Prayers of confession of sin (e.g. Pss. 51, 130)

Prayers for other people (e.g. Pss. 67, 72)

Prayers of self-dedication (e.g. Ps. 119)

Prayers of communion with God (e.g. Ps. 139)

Prayers of thanksgiving (e.g. Pss. 116, 130).

8. They show what the Israelites *believed about God*, e.g. that:

God is creator (Ps. 8);

God has chosen out a special People and has made a Covenant with them (Ps. 103.18)

God keeps his promises, i.e. He is "faithful" and "true" (Ps. 25)

God treats men with justice, He is "fair" (Ps. 98.9)

God saves and rescues His people from evil because of His "mercy" (Ps. 103.4–8)

God rules as King, and controls all nations (Ps. 98.6)
God hates sin, and punishes people (Ps. 146.9c)

9. They are *for congregations.*

The Psalms are not just for monks or just for clergy or just for trained choirs to sing. They are prayers which the ordinary people of a congregation can offer to God.

It is true that some of the Psalms are not suitable for use by a congregation. In some cases part of a psalm is suitable, but the rest is not. But many psalms provide exactly the sort of response which a Christian congregation wants to make to God.

Today Christians in many different countries are discovering ways in which congregations can use the Psalms. See General Note B, p. 116.

10. They are *for individuals.*

Often we find that a psalm contains just the words that we *want* for our prayer to God (as did the boy William Cowper). At other times a psalm will help us to find a better way of praying: e.g. a man who is in despair uses Psalm 42 as a prayer, and finds that it shows him how to put his confidence in God in spite of his troubles.

11. They are for *members of all Churches.*

There are no other songs and hymns which Christians from all parts of God's Church share. It is God's will that Christians should be united, and the Psalms are one great opportunity which God has given us of showing that we are one through Jesus Christ.

# Further comment on Psalm 118

## THEME

We have seen that this is a psalm of praise to God, and of thanksgiving for safety after trouble.

The plan of Psalm 118 is as follows:

**Vv. 1–4:** A singer calls on different groups of worshippers to praise God.

**Vv. 5–18:** A singer (perhaps the king) thanks God because He has rescued the people from their enemies.

**Vv. 19–22:** Thanksgiving to God as the procession reaches the gates of the Temple.

**Vv. 23–29:** Thanksgiving to God as the king passes through the gates ("he who enters" v. 26).

## USE

Christians use this psalm especially at Easter.

## NOTES

**Ps. 118.2, 3: Declare it, house of Israel . . . house of Aaron.** In these verses the singer first turns to the ordinary people ("house of Israel"), then to the priests ("house of Aaron"), and then to "those that fear the Lord". These last words probably mean the whole congregation of people and priests.

**Ps. 118.15: The tents of the righteous.** These words may refer to the little tents or "booths" which the worshippers used at the Feast of "Tabernacles" or Tents. At this festival they remembered how God had rescued them out of slavery and had cared for them during their years of wandering: "You shall dwell in booths for seven days . . . that your generations may know that I made the people of Israel dwell in booths when I brought them out of the land of Egypt" (Lev. 23.42).

**Ps. 118.22: The stone which the builders rejected has become the chief cornerstone.** I.e. God has chosen for a special purpose some person or a group of people who seemed small and unimportant.

We find the same sort of statement in other parts of the Bible. In this verse the people referred to as the "cornerstone" are the whole tribe of Israel. In parts of Isaiah it means the few Israelites who have remained faithful to God who are the "cornerstone" (see Isa. 10.20, 21). In Mark 12.10, 11 and Acts 4.11 it means Jesus Himself.

**Ps. 118.25, 26: Save us . . . Blessed be he who enters in the name of the Lord.** When the Israelites first used this psalm, they sang these verses as the king passed through the gates of the Temple. There were two sorts of prayer in their minds; first, a prayer that God would continue to save them from their enemies, and secondly, thanksgiving for His help in times past.

As Christians read these verses they remember that the crowds shouted them aloud as Jesus rode into Jerusalem on a donkey. "Those who went before and those who followed cried, 'Hosanna! Blessed be he who comes in the name of the Lord' " (Mark 11.9). Perhaps they used those words because it was the Feast of Tabernacles at the time, and because many people wanted to make Jesus a political leader to save the Jews from the Romans.

Some years after Jesus had ridden into Jerusalem, Christians began to realize that Jesus actually was the "Saviour" sent by God, i.e. that Jesus was doing for all mankind what the Israelites had asked God to do for them in Psalm 118. He was indeed "saving" mankind and He had indeed "entered the world in the name of the Lord".

Today Christian worshippers find these words appropriate at any time when they experience that Jesus is present amongst the fellowship of those who believe in Him.

*Note:* We have seen in this Introduction that the Israelites probably sang Psalm 118 after they had come back from exile, and that Jesus probably used it at the end of the last Supper. But although we can say that it is likely that the psalm was used at those times, there is no proof. For the other occasions, however, which are described above there are historical records. From these we *know* that Psalm 118 was used.

## STUDY SUGGESTIONS

### CONTENT

1. Many people think that Psalm 118 was sung:
   (a) By the Israelites after they had returned from exile,
   (b) by Jesus after the last Supper.
   For what reasons do people think this in each case?
2. For what reasons do you think Christians have chosen Psalm 118:
   (a) For early morning worship?
   (b) For an Easter service?
3. (a) From which verses in Psalm 118 can we see the *ways* in which the Israelites used it?
   (b) What were those ways?
4. What did the Israelites (a) remember, (b) do, at the Feast of Tabernacles?
5. In what place did the Israelites chiefly sing the Psalms?

### BIBLE

6. In what way are vv. 19 and 20 of Psalm 118 like vv. 7–10 of Psalm 24?
7. Which verses of Psalm 118 do we also find in Psalm 106, Psalm 107, and Ezra 3.11?
8. (a) What were the Israelites doing as they sang or shouted Ps. 118.26?
   (b) Who shouted the same words many years later, according to Mark 11.9?
   (c) Why did they use such words?
   (d) Why do some Christians use them in their services today?

### DISCUSSION AND RESEARCH

9. Give one reason why Christians use the Psalms today.
10. For what two chief reasons are the Psalms difficult for Christians to use today? Use Psalm 118 in giving your opinion.
11. What different ways of using the Psalms in Christian worship have you yourself experienced?

# The Crown
# Psalm 8

## THEME

### 1. THE EXPERIENCE: POWER

Even very small children know that they have power. By shouting loudly they can persuade their mothers to give them food. We may compare this with the experience of the head of a very large modern state, Russia, China, or USA, who has the power to destroy 100 million people and more by pressing a single button on his desk which is the signal that an atomic bomb is to be dropped. Somewhere between the experience of the ruler and that of the child lies the experience of us all.

We have such power over other living creatures that in some countries three-year-old children often drive herds of cattle, and human beings decide which animals, birds, and reptiles they will kill and which they will allow to live.

We have power over other people, and we become aware of it especially when we are older brothers and sisters, school prefects, parents, teachers, policemen, money-lenders, leaders in society.

We have power over the rest of nature, and this is the power which has increased so very quickly during the last 100 years. We can overcome the sea by flying over it, reduce disease by medicine, flatten mountains by bulldozers, and even reach the moon.

What does this power do to us? What sort of people do we become by having power?

(a) Some people become so "intoxicated" with their own power over things and over other people that they do not ask what effect they are having on those things or people. In one city a man became rich by owning and hiring out a large number of heavy wooden hand-carts which were pushed by young men through the streets. One day he learnt from a doctor that most of the men who did the pushing became invalids for the rest of their lives owing to over-strain. People are today killing whales to get the oil, and do not seem to care when, as a result of their action, some species of whales cease to exist. Perhaps people become arrogant in this way because they think of themselves as being different from nature rather than part of it.

(b) Other people who have great power become terrified. In an old Greek story, those who discovered how to make fire believed that by doing so they would make the gods jealous, and would therefore die. Today mankind has such power that many people live in fear that that power may lead to the destruction of the whole human race.

(c) There is a third way of living with power, the way which was taken by those who first used this psalm: namely, to look beyond the power to God who has lent it and to whom human beings are answerable.

## 2. THE RECOGNITION OF GOD

(a) First, the people who used this psalm saw God as the one who in His power was the creator of everything: "the work of *thy* fingers" (v. 3a), "the moon and the stars which *thou* hast established" (v. 3b), "*thou* hast made" (v. 5a). The power which we possess is only a part of the Power in which God gave existence to the world. See note on Psalm 100.3b.

(b) Secondly, they saw God as the "Sustainer", i.e. as One who in His power continued to create: "thou *dost* care" (v. 4), "thou *dost* crown" (v. 5b). God did not create the world and then leave it. We see this clearly also in Psalm 104: "thou *waterest* the mountains" (Ps. 104.13), "thou *dost* cause the grass to grow" (Ps. 104.14), "When thou *sendest* forth thy Spirit, they are created" (Ps. 104.30). So when a man and his wife come together and a child is conceived, they are uniting themselves with God the continuing creator.

(c) Thirdly, they saw God as "Delegator", i.e. that He delegates His authority and power to human beings. "Thou hast made him little less than God, and dost crown him . . ."; "Thou has given him dominion over the works of thy hands"; "Thou hast put all things under his feet" (vv. 5, 6). God has given human beings a special place in creation ("Thou dost crown him", v. 5). We are a part of nature, but God has appointed us to exercise responsible control over it. Because our appointment (or "commission" or "authority") has come from God, we are answerable to Him for the way in which we use this power.

This is the truth which we also read in Genesis 1.26–30, e.g. "God said, 'Let us make man in our image, after our likeness: and let them have dominion over the fish of the sea'" (Gen. 1.26). See note on Psalm 8.6.

Two words in Psalm 8 which show the truth about God which the Israelite worshippers had recognized are "name" and "glory". "How majestic is thy name" (v. 1a); "Thou whose glory above the heavens is chanted" (v. 1b). The Israelites used both these words to show that the great Creator God has chosen to enter into relationship with human beings. This means that human beings can in some way "know" Him, even though He is the Creator. See notes on p. 170.

These two words (and the truths behind them) were often used in the Temple services, e.g. in Psalm 145, "I will bless thy *name*" (v. 1), "All thy works shall . . . speak of the *glory* of thy kingdom" (vv. 10, 11). In the whole of Psalm 145 the worshippers praised God:

for His "greatness" (vv. 1–3),

for His activity (vv. 4–7),
for His "mercy" (vv. 8, 9),
for His sovereignty (vv. 10–13b), and
for His support to human beings (vv. 13c–20).

## 3. THE RESPONSE

This psalm expresses two different sorts of response which the worshippers made as a result of recognizing God.

(a) The first sort of response expressed in Psalm 8 is *dependence on God*. The worshippers felt weak and small in the presence of their Creator. "What is man?" (v. 4). See note on p. 71. Yet they did not only feel weak; they looked to God with gratitude, knowing that they depended on Him.

(b) The second sort of response is *acceptance of responsibility*. The worshippers did not only rejoice in the honour of being "crowned" (v. 5b). They also dedicated themselves as being responsible for looking after the earth over which God had given them dominion (v. 6). See note on p. 100.

The plan of Psalm 8 (the worshipper's response) is as follows:

V. 1a:   The chorus: Praise to God.
Vv. 1b–2:   God shows His power in creation and in overcoming evil.
Vv. 3–8:   Man is both dependent upon God and in a position of responsibility.
V. 9:   The chorus: Praise to God.

## USE

At first this psalm was probably the response of worshippers to the great truths about God which had been set forth in the Temple worship. The leaders of worship had set forth these truths in such ways as the carrying of the Ark of the Covenant in procession, and by referring to God's "Name" and to His "glory". A singer or a choir probably sang the "strophes" of the psalm (a "strophe" is a group of verses); then the congregation shouted or sang the chorus (v. 1 and v. 9) at the end of each strophe. In the chorus God is addressed as "*our* Lord".

This psalm is clearly suitable for congregational worship today, the people singing or shouting the chorus. In some Churches it is used at Christmas time, for the reason that Jesus Christ is the one human being who fully exercised the "dominion" and responsibility of which we read in v. 6. He was always answerable to God for the way He used His power: "I do nothing on my own authority" (John 8.28).

## NOTES

**Ps. 8.1a: O Lord, our Lord.** The word "Lord" is used in the RSV to

"We are a part of nature, but God has appointed us to exercise responsible control over it" (p. 10).

Two Chinese technicians are engaged in making a dam, so that barren mountainous country can be turned into farm-land, which will be as fertile, perhaps, as these well-cared for terraces in the Philippines.

translate two different Hebrew words. The first is the Hebrew name for God, *Yahweh*. The second is *Adonai*, which in other English versions is translated as "Master", "Governor", or (as in the NEB) "Sovereign". **Ps. 8.1b: How majestic is thy name.** When the Israelites spoke of God's "name", they had two chief ideas in mind:

1. They thought of God's *character*, as He has shown it to human beings. Sometimes they used the phrase "God's name" simply to mean "God". "Those who know thy name put their trust in thee" (Ps. 9.10).

2. They thought of God's *activity*, i.e. they thought of Him as doing the sort of things which you would expect from someone with that character. "Blessed be the Lord, the God of Israel, who alone does wondrous things. Blessed be his glorious name for ever." (Ps. 72.18, 19).

**Ps. 8.1b, 2: Thou whose glory ... is chanted by the mouth of babes ...** In some versions the translators have put a full stop after "chanted". The passage then becomes: "Thy glory above the heavens is chanted. By the mouths of babes thou hast founded a bulwark". According to Matthew 21.16 Jesus quoted Psalm 8 in this way: "Out of the mouth of babes and sucklings thou hast brought perfect praise."

The Israelites used the word "glory" in rather the same way as they used "name":

1. They thought of it as a special *showing forth* of the presence of God during Temple worship. "All the peoples behold his glory" (Ps. 97.6).

2. They thought of God's presence as a presence of power. We could compare this power to the power of a strong wind pressing heavily against a door. The Hebrew word *kabod* which is usually translated "glory" means "weight": "Ascribe to the Lord glory and strength" (Ps. 29.1b).

3. They thought of God's glory-in-power as shown in the *special things which he had done for the Israelites* in the past.

**Ps. 8.4a: What is man ... ?** As the worshippers felt their smallness and weakness in the presence of God, they knew that they depended upon Him.

A baby depends on its parents, a fish depends on water, and a tree depends on the air and soil around it. But mankind's dependence on God is even greater, because God is the maker and controller of all living things.

In these days we have so much knowledge and power that we can, for example, create great lakes by building dams like Kariba in Africa or the Hirakud dam in India which is sixteen miles long. Because of achievements like this, people may think that they have "grown up" so much that they no longer have any need for God. But we shall never cease to depend on God for our existence. If we respect the laws which He has laid down for the earth, there is life for us all. If we pretend that there is no Lord and no laws, there is disaster. Man is only great if he honours God as One who is greater.

The writers of many other psalms expressed this reverence for God's will and this dependence upon Him as Creator and Sustainer, e.g. "The heavens are telling the glory of God" (Ps. 19.1).

The whole of Psalm 104 is on this theme. In verses 1–9 the writer began by praising God the Creator: "Thou didst set the earth on its foundations" (v. 5). In verses 10–30 he praised God as the present Sustainer, e.g. "Thou makest springs gush forth" (v. 10). Then in verses 31–35 he looked forward to God's continuing His work of creating and sustaining, "May the glory of the Lord endure for ever" (v. 31). There is a doxology "Bless the Lord, O my soul" at the beginning and at the end of the psalm.

**Ps. 8.4: Thou art mindful . . . thou dost care.**

1. The Hebrew word which is translated as *mindful* in the RSV means more than remembering; it means that God does two things for His people:

(a) He rescues them from evil (this is the meaning of this verse);

(b) He corrects or "punishes" them when they go wrong. See Ps. 25.6, 7: "Be mindful of thy mercy, O Lord . . . Remember not . . . my transgressions."

The word which is translated as *care* in the RSV (and which is often translated as "visit") has a similar meaning: that God brings a change to people's lives. He either brings a welcome gift or He brings discipline and correction. In Psalm 65.9 we see that God's visit produces harvest; in Psalm 89.32 that God will "visit" the transgression of the Israelites "with a rod". God is always both loving and stern; and He is stern *because* He is loving.

2. As we study these two words, we can see that the thought which is expressed in v. 4 line 1 is repeated in line 2. The worshippers are saying the same thing twice over, and expressing it in different words.

We see the same kind of repetition in the strophe which follows: the truth that God has given human beings special responsibility is first stated in v. 5, and then it is stated again in different words in v. 6 (the second half of the strophe). The two parts of the strophe each say the same thing.

This special way of writing songs and hymns is often called "parallelism", because the two parts are "parallel". It is important to notice this in order to interpret the Psalm correctly. For example in v. 4 we might think that the "son of man" in 4b meant something different from "man" in 4a. But in the light of this special Hebrew way of writing, it is plain that this is not so; in both cases the meaning is "mankind", or "human beings".

In every language there are special customs as regards the writing of poetry. In English, for example, many poets have made the ends of their lines rhyme, e.g.:

> Hark! the herald angels *sing*
> "Glory to the new born *King*."

This was not a Hebrew custom. But the custom of parallelism was very common in Hebrew poetry. We have already noticed one sort of parallelism. And there are other sorts, e.g. when the poet expresses negatively in the second part of the verse or strophe what he had said positively in the first part, e.g.:

> "The Lord watches over the way of the righteous,
> But the way of the wicked is doomed."
> (Ps. 1.6, NEB)

**Ps. 8.6: Thou hast given him dominion . . .** God has not given us dominion and power to do what we choose with His world, but power to control nature on behalf of God. We are "responsible" for the earth, i.e. we must give account to God for the way we use it. What does "being responsible" mean?

It is responsible to cut down trees for firewood or for making into paper, but only if people first consider what the results will be, and if they take proper action to prevent any harm which may follow. E.g. they need to ask: How can we provide other protection from wind and rain, so that the top-soil is not washed away? Will the cutting down of large numbers of trees reduce the rainfall and cause famine? Where else will birds nest, the birds who eat the insects which spoil the crops?

It is right for people to use larger and faster aircraft, but only if they first consider such questions as: Will there be enough agricultural land if many acres are used for larger runways? If the nations spend a great deal of money on developing these new planes, will there be enough money left for developing hospitals and schools?

By taking such questions seriously, people show that they respect the laws by which God created the world.

## STUDY SUGGESTIONS

WORDS

1. "The word 'glory' was often used in Temple services" (p. 10).
   (a) (i) What sort of things do you describe as "glorious" in ordinary conversation? Make a list.
   (ii) If you said that someone received "glory", what would you mean by this?
   (b) Compare the meaning of the words "glorious" and "glory" as you have described it under (a) above, with the meaning of "glory"

15

as it is used in Psalm 8 concerning God.

2. (a) In which *two* of the following sentences does the word "name" have a similar meaning to its meaning in the chorus of Psalm. 8?
   (b) In what way is it similar?
      (i) The Chairman has a name for fairness.
      (ii) The name of this plant is Euphorbia.
      (iii) I felt I had disgraced my family's good name.
      (iv) If you suspect anyone here of lying, then name him!

3. What do the following words mean, as used in this study of Psalm. 8?
   (a) strophe      (b) parallelism

## CONTENT

4. It is not enough to say that God once created the world. What more do we need to say in order to state the truth more fully?

5. What two chief thoughts did the writer of Psalm 8 have when he spoke about God being "mindful"?

## BIBLE

6. Each of the following groups of passages contains an important truth about God which is also contained in Psalm 8.
   (a) What is the truth in each group?
   (b) In which verse of Psalm 8 do we find it?
      (i) Ps. 24.1, 2; Ps. 33.6, 7; Ps. 102.25; Ps. 146.6
      (ii) Ps. 65.7, 8; Ps. 135.6, 7; Ps. 145.14
      (iii) Gen. 1.26–28

7. "Man is great only if he honours God as One who is greater" (p. 14). In what way do the following verses support this statement?
   (a) Jer. 9.23–24      (b) 1. Cor. 1.31 and 15.10

8. In one sort of "parallelism" (see p. 14) the writer repeats, in the second part of a verse or strophe, the thought which he has expressed in the first part. Read the following passages, and say in each case what thought the writer has repeated:
   (a) Ps. 8.4a and 8.4b   (b) Ps. 9.1a and 9.1b   (c) Ps. 19.1   and 19.2
   (d) Ps. 27.1a and 27.1b   (e) Luke 1.46b and 1.47).

9. In vv. 10–30 of Psalm 104 the writer praised God as the "present sustainer", e.g. "Thou madest springs gush forth" (v. 10) (p. 14).
   (a) In what other phrases in Psalm 104 does the writer say the same thing?
   (b) Which of these phrases (in the same or similar words) are also used in Psalm 145?

## DISCUSSION AND RESEARCH

10. Give examples from your own experience, of:
    (a) The different sorts of power that people have;

(b) people being afraid of their own power.
11. Several examples are given on p. 15 of ways in which human beings can exercise "responsibility" in their use of the earth.
Give examples from your own experience, of:
(a) human beings accepting such responsibility
(b) human beings failing to accept it.
12. What would you reply to someone who said: "It is only a feeble and infantile person who needs to depend upon God?"
13. "God is always both loving and stern; and He is stern *because* He is loving." (p. 14)
How far has it been your experience that the second half of this statement is true? Give an example to explain your answer.
14. Psalm 8 has often been used as the basis of Harvest Festival services in the Church. Draw up an outline for such a service, remembering the need for members of the congregation to participate actively.

# Sweeter than Honey
## Psalm 19

## THEME

### 1. THE EXPERIENCE: ORDER

Before a baby is born, he is aware that his mother's heart beats regularly. The "beat" will be repeated: he can depend upon that. He has experienced one sort of "order". Later in his life he will have the same experience as he discovers that the light from the sun returns every day; that there is a "new moon" every 28 days; that his wife creates a new egg inside her womb every 28 days; that the green grass begins to shoot from the ground, or the ice begins to melt, at one particular time each year.

There are other kinds of "order", too, which we experience.

We discover that if we do *this*, *that* results. As babies we found that each time we fed from our mother we received a pleasant feeling. Later we have found that if we eat and sleep well we are fit for work the next day. If we do not watch the cars carefully as we cross the road we may be killed.

We notice that a tree produces another tree which has the same sort of leaf and the same sort of flower as the parent tree. We see that parent birds produce another bird which behaves just like the parents and looks just like them.

We see the orderly arrangement of created things. Each of our eyes is the same distance from our nose. Each hand has five fingers, and each foot five toes. We may have seen the eye of a dragon-fly through a microscope and discovered that there were 30,000 separate sections, each placed so as to receive light in its own way.

As children we saw that our parents had a special place in the family. Later we realized that each member of the family had his own special part to play. We saw that order existed when all members understood this. Later still we saw that, in the same way, order exists in a tribe or nation when each member accepts his own special place, and when each accepts some person or people as being in authority over the rest.

We see the same sort of "order" when we compare ourselves with other creatures. We human beings walk on two feet, but goats and cows walk on four. It takes 22 years for a human brain to become fully-grown, but a monkey's brain grows to its full size after only six months. Each sort of created thing behaves in its own special way.

We experience another sort of order when we see the sameness or unity in God's creation. Many sorts of animals, most birds, and even some reptiles and fishes are like human beings in the way they make nests or lairs where they can bring up their young in safety. They are like human beings in the way they need air to breathe.

The Israelites who used Psalm 19 in their worship were rejoicing in their experience of order. In this psalm they were thinking mainly of the first two sorts of order which are mentioned above, namely:

1. They could rely on some visible events being repeated regularly. The sun appeared every morning and the darkness gave them rest every night. "Day to day pours forth speech, and night to night declares knowledge" (v. 2); "The sun ... runs its course with joy" (v. 5).

2. They saw an orderly connection between what they did and what happened afterwards, i.e. if they worshipped "other gods" or behaved deceitfully in their selling of market produce, then trouble resulted. They called this "law", and they described it as being "sweeter than honey" (v. 10). They felt secure in the world and were free to live and work because they could rely upon this sort of "order" continuing.

## 2. THE RECOGNITION OF GOD

But the writers of this psalm were not simply describing order: they were seeing God as the giver of this order. "Order", they said, "is in God Himself. It is God who has made the world in such a way that we can see order and feel secure." There are several psalms in which this is the main theme. We have already studied Psalm 8. Another is Psalm 148, in which the writer invited all created things and people to serve and praise God because it was God who had given them the order by which they existed: "Praise him, sun and moon.. . . praise him all you shining stars . . . for He fixed their bounds which cannot be passed" (vv. 3 and 6b).

We may study the truth about God which the writer of Psalm 19 saw, by looking at five words which he used: glory, handiwork, law, rock, redeemer.

1. *Glory* (v. 1): See note on p. 13. This word means the "pressure" of God upon the world, pressure which is the reason for order in the universe.

2. *Handiwork* (v. 1b): Many peoples have believed that the sun is God, e.g. in Egypt. The Israelites on the other hand believed that God is apart from the universe. They believed that He is greater than it, and that the orderly way in which things happen is His handiwork. See note on Psalm 100.3b. Parsis in India (called Zoroastrians in Iran) give special reverence to fire and the sun today; a fire always burns in their places of worship. But they do not worship the sun or fire.

3. *Law* (v. 7): As we shall see below (note on Psalm 103.18) the "law" of the Lord means the guidance which God gives concerning human living. God says: "This is how I made you. Live like this and you will find peace."

4. *Rock* (v. 14c): When the writer used this word he was praising God because He is unchangeable. For a fuller study of "rock", see note on p. 52.

5. *Redeemer* (v. 14c): There are two important Hebrew words which are often translated "redeem". One is *padhah* (see note on Psalm 130.8b); the other is *gaal* which is used here. Those who used this word *gaal* (rather than *padhah*) were thinking of the close personal relationship between God and His People. They were saying three further things about God:

(a) Although He is the unchangeable Creator of order and law, He is also the rescuer of those who fail to keep the law. "I have swept away your transgressions . . . Return to me for I have redeemed you" (Isa. 44.22).

(b) God, not human beings, has taken the first step in this rescue. "Fear not, for I *have* redeemed you" (Isa. 43.1).

(c) God offers to rescue the whole people of Israel, not simply individuals. "You men of Israel . . . your Redeemer is the Holy One of Israel" (Isa. 41.14).

For a study of words which writers of the Psalms used to describe God's rescue of Israel, see note on Psalm 22.21.

## 3. THE RESPONSE

Psalm 19, which is the response of the worshippers to God, consists of two songs of praise, with a personal prayer at the end.

Vv. 1–6: First song—Praise to God the Creator: (a) God is Creator of

"The Israelites who used Psalm 19 were rejoicing in their experience of 'order' " (p. 18).

The first drops of rain are a sign of life for the people of Taiwan. They can rely on the rain coming at the same times each year. Because they experience order in this way, they prepare by ploughing the rice fields to make them ready for planting.

all creation (vv. 1–4b); (b) God is Creator of the order which the movements of the sun demonstrate (vv. 4c–6).

**Vv. 7–10:** Second song—Praise to God, the Creator of the order which His "Law" demonstrates.

**Vv. 11–14:** Prayer—A personal request for God's help in overcoming sin.

## USE

1. It may be that there were once two psalms (vv. 1–4b and vv. 4c–14) which an editor put together much later. (The Hebrew name for God is *El* in vv. 1–4b, and is *Yahweh* in vv. 4c–14. Also the rhythm of the words is different in the two parts.)

But it is clear that those who used it, whether as one psalm or two, used it during the Temple services. Perhaps it was used at the time of the morning sacrifice, as the sun rose.

2. The theme of the psalm is that the will of God is not hidden, but is revealed to mankind, through the creation and the "law". For this reason Christians have often used this psalm at Christmas time. At Christmas Christians celebrate the will or "Word" of God being made known to human beings in a special way, i.e. in Jesus Christ. "In the beginning was the Word . . . He was in the beginning with God . . . And the Word became flesh and dwelt among us . . . And we have seen His glory . . ." (John 1.1, 2, 14).

## NOTES

**Ps. 19.1: The heavens . . . the firmament.** When the writer used the word "heavens", he meant the part of the sky and the atmosphere which he could see with his eyes. He used the word "firmament" to describe a hard roof which he thought covered the world. On this roof he believed there was an ocean of water which came to human beings as rain through windows in the roof.

When we use the words today we think of a universe which is so large, according to scientists, that it seems to have no limits. There are objects like stars called "quasars" which are so far away that their light, travelling at 180,000 ft a second, has taken 5,000 million years to reach us. In other words, their light is the light from an explosion which took place at the same time as our earth began. Through the discoveries of scientists, therefore, we have even more reason than the writer of Psalm 19 had to speak of the greatness of God the creator.

**Ps. 19.1b: The firmament proclaims his handiwork.** But does the firmament "proclaim" God? Do people believe in God because they have studied the orderly behaviour of stars? Some readers of Psalm 19 today feel that the writers, in their response to God, were too childish in their thinking. These readers ask important questions such as the following:

Did the writers not see disorder as well as order around them? Had they never sat with a man or woman whose only son had just been killed? (At the time when Israelites sang this psalm a Hindu hymn-writer was singing about the goddess Kali: "All creation is the sport of my mad mother Kali.")

Did the writers not experience that those who "keep the law" do not always find peace, but instead often find pain?

Did they really think that the orderliness of events, such as the regular rising of the sun, proved that there was a God who directed these events?

As we do not know what the writers of Psalm 19 would reply, it is helpful to read what is written in other parts of the Old Testament, e.g. in the Book of Job. In reply to questions such as these, Job's answer was:

1. I too have found disorder and suffering. "Let the day perish wherein I was born" (Job 3.3). I too have seen that those who suffer do not always suffer because they did wrong. On the contrary those who do wrong are often successful people: "Why do the wicked . . . grow mighty in power?" (Job 21.7).

2. In spite of this I have seen enough order in the world to believe that there is order in God and that He is the creator of order. "The Lord answered . . . Where were you when I laid the foundation of the earth? . . . Who shut in the sea with doors . . . ?" (Job 38.1, 4, 8).

3. The order which I see in created things does not *prove* that God exists. Nor does disorder in the world prove that He does not exist. But the order which I see is the sign and symbol of the God whom I still trust. "My eye sees thee" (Job 42.5).

**Ps. 19.5: The sun comes forth like a bridegroom.** Among tribes whom the Israelites knew there was a traditional folk-story about a sun-god. In this story the god rested in the sea at night, lying in the arms of his bride, and went off to work each morning. The writer of Psalm 19 does not tell this story as if it was true, for as we have seen he did not think that the sun was God. But he did use it as an illustration of a truth, i.e. the truth that the sun has orderly movements.

Christians, similarly, are free to use traditional folk-stories to illustrate a truth which has been revealed through Jesus Christ. The Fon people of Dahomey in West Africa have a story about the god Mawu. This god sent his son Lisa to earth with a metal sword, with which he cut down parts of the forest. Lisa then explained to human beings that they would not survive unless they learnt from him how to make metal tools. With such tools they could get wood for making ploughs and building houses. A Christian teacher could use this story to illustrate the truth that Jesus Christ came into our world that we may "have life and have it abundantly" (John 10.10).

**Ps. 19.7: The law of the Lord is perfect.** The Hebrew word which is translated "law" here is one of six words which the writer uses to describe the guidance which God gives to human beings, or His "will" which in many different ways He reveals to them. We find the five other words in vv. 7–10.

The Hebrew word is *torah*. The Israelites used it in three chief ways:

1. Information which they obtained by magical means, e.g. by drawing lots. See Deuteronomy 33.8–10.

2. All the instructions and laws which God gave the Israelites, mainly instruction given through the priests. "Ask the priests concerning the law" (Hag. 2.11 AV).

3. Much later they used the word to describe the first five books of the Bible, the books which we often call the Pentateuch. "Everything written about me in the law of Moses" (Luke 24.44).

In this psalm the word "law" means God showing human beings the orderliness which is in creation. It means God showing them "how things work", as some agricultural teachers might say, "You'll find that you get the biggest crop from your coffee plants if you cut back all the shoots except five". This is why the writer delights in it (v. 8a), and why he calls it "true" (v. 9b).

It does not mean "the way that God likes things to be done", as if God were a schoolteacher telling the new boys in his class to "write their names at the top of the left hand margin not the right". Nor is it a list of duties. For these reasons "law" is not a good translation.

Many writers of the Psalms were praising God for this "guidance" e.g. in Psalms 1, 15, 111, 112, 119. These psalms are both acts of worship and notes of instruction to learners. They are often called "Wisdom psalms", because they are like other Wisdom writings, e.g. the Book of Proverbs. In Psalm 1, for example, the writer was showing in verses 1–3 that a man achieves the best life by keeping the law. "He is like a tree planted by streams of water" (v. 3). Then in verses 4–6 he showed that disaster comes when people disregard God's guidance (the "law").

Psalm 119 is a very long psalm, so long that Christians often use one or two sections at a time, e.g. vv. 97–112. But it is of the same sort as Psalms 1 and 24:

(a) It is partly thanksgiving because God has shown the "law" to His people. "Oh, how I love thy law" (v. 97). Eight different words are used to describe the law.

(b) It is partly a worshipper's cry to God:

(i) For help to be more loyal to Him: "Teach me, O Lord" (v. 33).

(ii) For protection against enemies: "Look on my affliction" (v. 153).

(c) It is partly instruction concerning right and wrong, and there are many comparisons between God's law and false ways, e.g. v. 29.

4. If the law was such an excellent thing, why did St Paul tell his readers to be "led by the spirit and not to be under the law" (Gal. 5.18)? The answer is that very many Jews had false ideas about the law:

(a) Some of them had come to think of "law" as only a list of rules which they could read in a book. They had forgotten that law or *torah* was the guidance of the living God.

(b) They had chosen some of the rules and called them "important", and had forgotten the others.

(c) As a result they became easily satisfied with their own achievements.

(d) They despised people who failed to keep these "important" rules. See Matthew 23.

**Ps. 19.9b: The ordinances of the Lord are true.** The Hebrew word translated "ordinances" is *mishpat.* Writers in the Old Testament use it in the following ways:

(a) The decision or ruling or judgement which a judge gives in court. "You shall not be partial in judgement" (Deut. 1.17).

(b) The decisions which God gives, as part of the guidance that He gives His people. This is its meaning in this verse and in Psalm 119.175 "Let thy ordinances help me".

(c) God's decision which men see to be just. "Shall not the Judge of all the earth do right" (Gen. 18.25). In this verse and in many others it is best to translate *mishpat* as "right" or "justice".

(d) Human behaviour which is right and just, i.e. which is of the same sort as God's treatment of His people. "He leads the humble in what is right" (Ps. 25.9).

It is clear from the above that the translation "judgement" which the AV usually gives is often misleading.

**Ps. 19.11: In keeping them there is great reward.** In saying this the writer was repeating the thought of earlier verses, such as "the ordinances of the Lord are true" (v. 9). It is as if the pupils of an agricultural class took the teacher's advice about growing coffee and found by experience that it was true. They really did have an increased crop the next year! It is as if a Christian were to say "It is worth being a Christian.'

St Paul also was thinking of order, the order of God's creation, when he wrote that "each one may receive good or evil, according to what he has done" (2 Cor. 5.10). And Jesus had said the same thing when He said, "He who believes has eternal life" (John 6.47). To say that "there is great reward", therefore, is to recognize a fact: the fact that God has created order in the world.

But we human beings have often forgotten that rewards are a fact. We have used them as the *chief* reason for our behaving well. When we do this we lose our sense of obedience to God. We feel that we can claim a reward from Him. We treat Him as if He were a bookseller who must hand us the books we want as soon as we have paid for them. This was the attitude to God which St Paul called "the works of the law" (Gal. 3.2). Paul expressed the true Christian attitude when he said, "It is by His grace you are saved, through trusting Him; it is not your own doing" (Eph. 2.8).

**Ps. 19.12, 13: Hidden faults . . . presumptuous sins.** The writer asked God for help so that these sins might not overwhelm him. He described two sorts of sins:

(a) Those which he himself did not notice in himself, "hidden faults". Everyone has hidden faults. One man despises people who have less money than he has; one woman makes someone else take the blame when people criticize her. But if neither of them know that they behave in that way, then neither of them can overcome their faults.

(b) Those which he knew that he committed. These faults are called "sins of pride" in most modern translations. (The RSV translation is "presumptuous sins".) This kind of "presumptuous pride" is a pretence. When I am proud in the presence of God I am pretending that I know better than He does. When I am proud in the presence of other people I am pretending that my own power has made me what I am.

*Note:* the word "pride" is used in two ways which we need to distinguish: (i) It refers to a fault and a weakness, as we have seen. (ii) It refers to something which everyone needs to have, i.e. self-respect.

**Ps. 19.14: Let the words . . . be acceptable in thy sight.** These words may remind us of the words which writers use to describe the sacrifice offered by a priest, e.g. in Leviticus 1.3 "that he may be accepted before the Lord".

In this psalm the writer was expressing two thoughts:

1. That he had no claim upon God, for God was not forced to listen to his prayer.

2. That, on the other hand, he had confidence in God, for God does in His goodness receive the prayers of human beings.

It is these two thoughts which Christians have in mind when they use such verses as the following in public worship: "Lord, hear our prayer and let our cry come unto thee" (Ps. 102.1) and "Lord, have mercy upon us."

## STUDY SUGGESTIONS

WORDS

1. The Israelites who used Psalm 19 were rejoicing in their experience of "order" (p. 18). Which *six* of the following words mean the opposite or nearly the opposite of "order":

muddle  death  chaos  disharmony  omission  confusion
contrast  noise  irregularity  luck

2. The word "pride" can be used in two different ways: (a) presumptuous pride (b) self-respect (see p. 25). Which four of the following words have the same or nearly the same meaning as (a), and which four have the same or nearly the same meaning as (b)?
conceit  vanity  courage  boasting  confidence  obstinacy
boldness  independence

3. Read again the note on "ordinances" (Hebrew *mishpat*) on p. 24. How is the word *mishpat* translated in the RSV in each of the following verses in the Psalms:
(a) 9.7b  (b) 18.22a  (c) 25.9a  (d) 33.5a  (e) 35.23a  (f) 37.6b
(g) 72.2b  (h) 97.8c  (i) 106.3a  (j) 119.175b?

4. What are the six words used in Psalm 19.7–10 to describe the guidance which God gives to human beings?

## CONTENT

5. The writer of Psalm 19 gave thanks to God for two sorts of order. What were these two sorts?

6. (a) What did the writer say was sweeter than honey?
(b) Why did he value it so highly?

7. What request did the writer of Psalm 19 make to God?

8. What did the writer mean by the word "firmament"?

9. Give one reason why St Paul told his readers "to be led by the spirit and not to be under the law"?

## BIBLE

10. What sort of "order" or "orderliness" is described in each of the following passages?
(a) Gen. 8.22  (b) Matt. 5.45  (c) Mark 4.30–32
(d) Luke 21.29, 30  (e) 1 Cor. 12.4–11  (f) Gal. 6.7

11. It has been shown in this chapter that the word "law":
(a) Sometimes refers to a helpful thing, i.e. to the guidance which God offers to His People that they may have the fullest life;
(b) At other times refers to a dangerous thing e.g. to a list of rules, which is dangerous because by keeping such rules people forget that they depend upon God's grace.
Read the following passages and say in each case whether the word is used with the meaning of (a) or (b) above:
(i) Ps. 19.7  (ii) Isa. 1.10  (iii) Matt. 5.17  (iv) Rom. 3.28
(v) Rom. 7.6  (vi) Rom. 7.12  (vii) Rom. 7.22  (viii) Gal. 3.2
(ix) Gal. 5.4

12. Read Psalm 148. What two truths about God does it contain, which Psalm 19 also contains?

13. (a) Read Psalms 1 and 119.1–8. What two thoughts do we find in both passages?
(b) Which verses of Psalm 19 are most like Psalm 119.1–8, and in what way are they like?

DISCUSSION AND RESEARCH

14. (a) In what three ways have you experienced "order" in the universe, in addition to the ways referred to in this chapter?
(b) It is said (p. 22) that if someone endures great suffering he may find it difficult to see order in the universe. For what other reasons do you think people find it difficult to see order?
15. Compare Psalm 19.11, "In keeping thy ordinances there is great reward", with the prayer of St Ignatius Loyola: "Teach us, good Lord, to serve Thee as thou deservest, to give and not to count the cost, to toil and not to seek for rest, to labour and not to ask for any reward except that of knowing that we do Thy will." In what way is the thought behind one like or unlike the thought behind the other?
16. "Cleanse thou me from hidden faults" (Ps. 19.12b).
What two things can a Christian do in order to discover his own faults which are "hidden" from him?
17. "Order exists in a tribe or nation when each member accepts his own special place, and when each accepts some one or some people as being in authority over the rest" (p. 18).
(a) What is your opinion of this?
(b) What two things make it difficult for this kind of order to exist today?

# The Mouth of the Lion
## Psalm 22

### THEME

1. THE EXPERIENCE: SUFFERING

The Christian Church in the southern Sudan has endured great sufferings in recent years, especially in the villages of the Nuer people. At one time, one of the ministers, after being released from a year's imprisonment and torture, wrote as follows to a friend: "There is much murdering and killing. You remember that little chapel at Nasir is near the army camp, so this is where they capture most of the people. We pray and ask God to help us, but there is no answer."

Such suffering is not only difficult to bear. It leads the sufferer also to doubt whether God can be in control and whether He cares. Suffering of this kind is near to despair.

Sometimes it is a single person who suffers, though others may give sympathy. A woman in India waited seven years to marry a man while he was receiving medical training overseas; but as he flew back to marry her his plane crashed and he was killed. A child felt that her parents did not want her. A young man beginning his career was told that he had contracted a long and painful disease.

Sometimes, as in the story from the Sudan, a whole group shares the experience.

It is clear from the words of Psalm 22 that this psalm was born out of experience of that kind. First we see the misery itself, which is mostly described in picture-language:

*weakness:* "I am a worm, and no man" (v. 6)

*isolation:* "All who see me mock at me" (v. 7)

*fears* as terrible as the fear of any wild animals or thieves: "a ravening and roaring lion" (v. 13); "they divide my garments" (v. 18)

*illness:* "I am poured out like water" (v. 14).

Secondly, the sufferer is confused, as often happens. After the terrible cyclone in the Bay of Bengal in 1970 a woman who had lost her husband and seven out of her eight children was so confused that she threatened to kill her own mother. So the writer of Psalm 22 seems not to know who to think about, whether himself, or his enemies, or God, and his thoughts run from one to the other.

Thirdly, he doubts whether God can any longer care about him (v. 1). A Christian girl of 19 living in London was friendly with a man and expected to marry him. One day she was knocked down by a bus and was told she would never use her right arm again. While she was in hospital she could not believe that a good God existed. For three years she called herself an "atheist". But today she is a member of the Church and married to the man she had been friendly with.

When people have to bear such desolation, what follows? It is easy for them to be full of pity for themselves, and thus to become a burden to those who live with them. Or they may despair completely so that they can see no reason for going on living.

Or they may be able to live through the present misery because they can still, so to speak, "hold to God with one finger". This is what the sufferer whose experience is described in Psalm 22 was able to do.

## 2. THE RECOGNITION OF GOD

1. First of all, in the middle of the writer's agony he was able to hold on to the simple fact that God exists. This is what a woman in Mombasa in Kenya was able to do. She was the only Christian in her family. At a time when she believed that her husband would soon ask to be baptized,

he fell from a coconut tree and was killed. She did not attend the pagan funeral rites, and as a result the rest of the family refused to visit her. They said there was a curse on anyone who had not shared in the burial. During this time two members of the Church gave her support and helped her to keep her belief in God's love.

2. Secondly, the writer was able to remember that God had sustained all His people in the past, including himself. "Thou art holy" (v. 3, see note below); "In thee our fathers trusted; . . . and thou didst deliver them" (v. 4); "Thou didst keep me safe upon my mother's breasts" (v. 9). God has "saved", "delivered", and "rescued" in the past, and He can do so again. (See note on v. 21 below, on these three words.) It was indeed part of the purpose of the Temple services in Israel to support the faith of the worshippers by reminding them of this. The leaders regularly reminded the worshippers that God had a special agreement or "Covenant" with His people. They used to tell the history of the Israelites, to show that God had kept His promises to them.

*Note:* God is called *"holy"* in v. 3. Here are three truths which the Israelites had in mind when they called God "holy":

1. God is great, powerful and even dangerous. According to 1 Samuel 6.19, 20, the Israelites believed that God was in a special way present wherever the Ark of the Covenant was present. They must have regarded the Ark (and God) with the same seriousness and awe with which we regard high-tension electric cable today, because we know its great power.

2. God is stern in His calling upon His people to behave with justice and mercy. "The Lord of hosts is exalted in justice, and the Holy God shows himself holy in righteousness" (Isa 5.16).

3. God is different and distinct from human beings, but He is not removed from them. We cannot say that "holy" simply means "separated". "Thus says the high and lofty One . . . whose name is Holy: 'I dwell in the high and holy place, and also with him who is of a contrite and humble spirit' " (Isa. 57.15).

We may note that the word "holy" was also used to describe the Israelites, because God called them, as He has also called the Christian Church, to be distinct from the world but not removed from it. See John 17.17–19.

## 3. THE RESPONSE

1. The first response to the experience of suffering expressed in this Psalm is a complaint to God (vv. 1–21) "My God, my God, why hast thou forsaken me?" (v. 1).

It may seem irreverent or even blasphemous of the sufferer to show his anger and frustration towards God in this way. But the worshipper who can pray like this makes some important discoveries:

(a) By expressing feelings of anger towards God he is less likely to hurt other people with his anger.

(b) He draws nearer to God with his complaints than if he turns away in silence. If he is angry with God, or hates Him, it is far better to tell God so, than to try to hide such feelings from Him.

(c) God Himself is well able to receive prayers of complaint. They cannot harm Him.

So St Teresa of Avila, having for the second time fallen into a stream (with all her clothes on), complained freely to God, "It is no wonder, God, that you have so few friends, if this is the way you treat them."

2. Secondly, it was a response of hope in God. Although he was suffering, in vv. 22–31 the worshipper spoke as if God had already rescued him: "He has not despised or abhorred the affliction of the afflicted" (v. 24). He could do this because of the way in which God had rescued others. See note on Psalm 42.5.

We may note two other psalms in which the writers complained to God and yet at the same time expressed their hope and trust in Him, Psalms 31 and 40.

In Psalm 31, the first part (vv. 1–18) is mainly a cry to God to rescue people from sickness (v. 10), from enemies (v. 11), and from sudden death (v. 13). The second part (vv. 19–24) is very like Psalm 22.22–31, i.e. it is prayer of such trust in God that the writer thanks God as though He had already rescued him ("Thou *didst* hear my supplication", v. 22).

But the two sorts of prayer go side by side throughout Psalm 31, e.g. in vv. 1–5 (which are often used as a separate psalm) we note "Rescue me speedily" (v. 2), and also "Thou hast redeemed me" (v. 5).

In Psalm 40, the prayer of thanks and hope is at the beginning, e.g. "I waited patiently for the Lord and He heard my cry" (v. 1). The cry for help is in the second half (vv. 11–17).

3. Finally the sufferer calls his fellow-worshippers, and all human beings, to praise God: "All the ends of the earth shall remember" (v. 27).

Psalm 22 consists of three sections of similar length:

**Vv. 1–11:** The sufferer's complaint to God.

**Vv. 12–21:** A description of his sufferings.

**Vv. 22–31:** His hope in God.

## USE

1. Perhaps this psalm (or part of it) was at first the prayer of an individual who was in trouble. But later on it probably came to be used in a public festival at which the king led the worship on behalf of the whole people of Israel. Possibly he dramatized in some symbolic

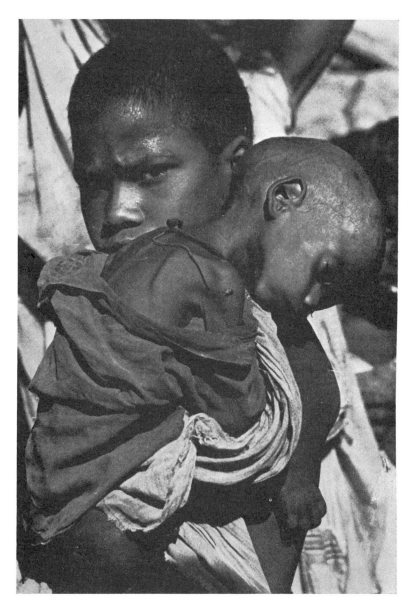

"My God, my God, why hast thou forsaken me?" (Ps. 22.1).

This little boy is carrying his baby brother, who is dying of starvation. During a recent famine, most of the babies in the area were in the same condition.

**What are the boy's thoughts? What if anything can Christians say or do for him?**

31

and ritual way the experience of being first humiliated and later restored by God. (Israelites had certainly experienced this often.)

2. Because Jesus Christ himself used words from this psalm when He was on the cross (Mark 15.34), Christians have mainly used it as a way of publicly remembering His death, e.g. on Good Friday.

3. The third part (vv. 22–31) is sometimes used separately. It is no dishonour to God to praise Him with part rather than the whole of a psalm. This part is a splendid congregational act of praise.

4. For someone praying alone this psalm is perhaps more of a guide than a passage to be spoken line by line. See Study Suggestion 15 on p. 35.

## NOTES

**Ps. 22.1: My God, my God, why hast thou forsaken me?**

1. We have already seen that Jesus used these words when He was dying. Here we may notice two important facts:

(a) Nothing in the Gospels shows us more clearly than this that Jesus was really man and that He really suffered. He suffered in body and in mind. His Father seemed to have left Him. But as we have seen, it was not a shout of complete despair. For Jesus, as for all Jews, Psalm 22 was a psalm of hope in God as well as a cry of distress.

(b) God, whom we see in Jesus Christ, is not distant from us; He is with us in our sufferings. Perhaps it is in this respect that the Christian conviction about God is different from other religious beliefs.

2. Jesus used this psalm because the Book of Psalms had always been His hymn-book and prayer-book, as it was for all Jews. Other occasions when He used psalms are the following:

Children greeted Him as He rode into Jerusalem and He spoke about the infants who praised God (see Ps. 8.1, 2 and Matt. 21.16);

He spoke of Himself as the stone which the builders would not use (see Ps. 118.22, 23 and Matt. 21.42);

He remembered the children's greeting and spoke about it (see Ps. 118.26 and Matt. 23.39);

He was teaching the Pharisees about the Messiah (see Ps. 110.1 and Matt. 22.44);

He prayed to God before He was arrested (see Ps. 6.4 and John 12.27);

At the Last Supper He said that one of His friends would betray Him (see Ps. 41.9 and John 13.18);

At the time of His death He entrusted Himself to His Father (see Ps. 31.5 and Luke 23.46).

**Ps. 22.7: "They wag their heads"** (compare Matt. 27.39–44). This is one of several phrases which we also find in the Gospel story of the suffering and death of Jesus. The others are in v. 1, v. 8, v. 15, v. 18. Are these verses in Psalm 22 a prediction of Jesus?

Some people believe that God miraculously inspired the writer of this psalm to predict the coming of Jesus and His suffering.

Others have gone further, and said that they could not believe in God unless they thought that God did miracles of this kind.

Others would say that in their experience God does not work in this way. He does not inspire people by miraculously putting His own knowledge in the place of theirs. He inspires them by moving them to dedicate their own knowledge to His service. According to this view, the story in the Gospels is like this psalm in some ways, because the Gospel writers knew the psalm very well indeed, and naturally used some of the familiar phrases when writing the Gospel.

Readers must work out their own interpretation.

**Ps. 22.15c: Thou dost lay me in the dust.** The writer believed that God Himself had sent this suffering. Is this true? Is suffering sent by God?

Three ideas which we find in the Old Testament are:

(a) That because God is creator, it is He who sends everything that happens. He sends both good and bad. (Job 2.10.)

(b) That suffering is always a punishment for sin. (Job 4.7.)

(c) That suffering is *not* always a punishment for sin. The book of Job was written partly in order to say this.

Among Christians we find the following ideas:

(a) That God has allowed suffering to happen and knows that it will happen, but that He does not "send" it. What He sends is His help to the sufferers.

(b) That when someone is ill it is not always the result of sin. (See John 9.3 and Luke 13.1–5.)

(c) That suffering often is the result of sin. Many people are suffering from syphilis or alcoholism or loneliness or remorse because of their own sin.

(d) That people often suffer as the result of other people's sins. A worker among Pakistani refugees in India wrote that "children were dying of cholera because the supplies of medicine and food had been stolen."

(e) That we who believe that God loves people will never fully understand why there is so much suffering. We believe in God in faith and in spite of suffering.

**Ps. 22.21: Save me.** The Israelites asked God to save them because they believed that He loved them and had the power to help them. But not all human beings have thought that God saves: e.g. the Greeks believed that many of the gods were cruel, and played tricks on people. Siva, a Hindu god, is feared because he is believed to bring illness and death.

There are many different Hebrew words which writers of the Psalms used to describe ways in which God sends help. In the RSV these are translated by such words as:

Save. See note on Psalm 67.2.

Redeem. See notes on Psalms 19.14 and 130.8.

Restore. See notes on Psalms 23.3 and on p. 61.

Heal. See note on Psalm 103.3b.

Forgive. See note on Psalm 130.4a.

Deliver. See Psalms 91.3, 14 and 116.8.

**Ps. 22.22: I will praise thee.** This verse is the beginning of the new section, in which the writer expresses hope in God.

We have said that the whole of Psalm 22 is the complaint of someone who nevertheless was able to hope in God. We should note here that some people interpret it differently: they say that it was always a thanksgiving. In this case the writer was remembering his past suffering in vv. 1–21, and offering thanksgiving in vv. 22–31.

## STUDY SUGGESTIONS

### WORDS

1. (a) Which *four* of the following words describe the experience from which Psalm 22 arose?
   desolation   denial   misery   agony   death   decision   suffering
   (b) Suggest another word which could be added to those four.
2. We read above of "words used to describe ways in which God sends help". What four words of this kind are used in Psalm 22?

### CONTENT

3. What thought helped the writer of Psalm 22 to hold to his belief in God?
4. What do people experience after they have freely expressed their anger or frustration to God?
5. (i) On what occasion did Jesus use words from Psalm 22?
   (ii) On what occasions did Jesus quote the following?
       (a) Ps. 8.1, 2   (b) Ps. 31.5   (c) Ps. 41.9

### BIBLE

6. In what two ways is Psalm 22 like Psalms 16 and 57?
7. Read Matthew 27.35–46 and John 19.25–37. These passages describe four occasions when the sufferings of Jesus seem to have been like the sufferings described in Psalm 22. Say in each of the four instances:
   (a) What suffering is described.
   (b) Which verse of Psalm 22 refers to similar suffering.

8. (a) Read Psalm 31.19–24. In what way is this passage like Psalm 22.22–31?
(b) Are either of these passages suitable for use in Christian worship? If so, in what way can they be used?
(c) Which other parts of Psalm 22 are suitable for use in public worship, and in what way?
9. Read Psalm 40.11–17. Which part of Psalm 22 is like that passage, and in what way?
10. What did the writers of each of the following passages say about God when they call Him "holy"?
Psalm 99.3 and 4   Isaiah 8.13   Hosea 11.9

DISCUSSION AND RESEARCH

11. (a) Give four examples of "picture-language" used in this Psalm.
(b) Why do you think the writer used "picture-language"?
12. "Several verses which refer to suffering in this psalm . . . we also find in the Gospel story of the suffering and death of Jesus. Are these verses in Psalm 22 a prediction of Jesus? Or was it by chance that the same things happened to Jesus?" (pp. 32, 33)
What is your own answer to those questions?
13. In Psalm 22.1 and 10 we read "My God", but Jesus taught His disciples to say "*Our* Father".
(a) To what extent does your Church keep "I" and "my" for private prayer, and "we" and "our" for public worship, e.g. in the hymns, creeds, prayers?
(b) Give your own opinion on what is done.
14. "God can help the sufferer to use his suffering". In a discussion on this subject two opinions were expressed:
(a) "It is true. A Christian needs to suffer in order to discover how much he needs God."
(b) "It is a dangerous thing to say. It makes people think that God's position depends on people being weak and in trouble, and that He is jealous when they are strong and prosperous."
What is your opinion?
15. A cleaner in Paris found an old exercise book which had been thrown away. The following is a translation of what was written in French on the back page:
"O God, have you forgotten me? In this city no one cares what happens to me. Fellow-students make jokes against me. I am having pains in my chest again. My health is failing and I am afraid of what may happen. This affects my work and I have my exams in June. My tutor looks at me as if he knows I shall fail. O God, do you not care? Why did you bless me so much before and leave me now?"

(a) In what ways are the words of the person who wrote this prayer (i) like, and (ii) unlike Psalm 22?
(b) What do you think could have most helped that person (see Psalm 22.7)?
16. "If he is angry with God . . . it is far better to tell God so, than to hide such feelings from Him" (p. 30).
What is your opinion?
17. "Not all human beings have thought that God saves" (p. 33). What people do you know, or have you read about, who do not believe that God saves? What do they believe about Him?
18. Give an example from everyday life of someone suffering because of the sins of others.

# The Shepherd
# Psalm 23

## THEME

### 1. THE EXPERIENCE: UNCERTAINTY

Some years ago, three American astronauts who were on their way to land on the moon reported that something had gone wrong with their space-ship. It was doubtful if they would be able to return to earth alive. The wives and families of the men received this news on their radios and had to wait nearly a week before they heard that the danger was over.

A mother, whose first baby died of typhoid fever, is nursing her second child who has fallen ill. The doctor says that this child also has typhoid.

A Jamaican politician has recently expressed disagreement with the party to which he belongs. He did so through conscience. Now he hears that the party officials may dismiss him from membership. He feels that if this happens his whole career will be ruined.

A student in Korea, having failed twice in an important examination, is preparing to sit the examination for the third and last time.

All those people were in situations of uncertainty and worry. Those who first used Psalm 23 had experienced the distress and pain of such uncertainty, as we see from the words "shadow" (v. 4) and "enemies" (v. 5).

Whole communities, as well as individuals, have this experience too. The inhabitants of a village in the Middle East have lived for ten years and more knowing that fighting between Israel and Jordan might at any time break out and lead to their homes being destroyed and them-

36

selves being killed. Indeed most of the inhabitants of the world today know that if one country uses atomic weapons and another country fights back in the same way, it may result in the destruction of the whole human race.

What do people actually do? How can people endure such uncertainty and worry? Often they allow their worries to overwhelm them. From being worried, they become anxious; and anxiety can become an illness of the mind. It can, for instance, seriously prevent us from living usefully or actively, for anxiety divides the mind. But there is something else people can do: They can recognize God as active in such situations.

## 2. RECOGNITION OF GOD

Those who created this psalm show that in such situations it is possible to recognize God as active:

(a) in guiding people (see "shepherd" v. 1, "leads" v. 3b).

(b) in offering people a fresh start (see "restores" v. 3a).

(c) in giving people what they need in order to do what He wills (see "rod and staff" v. 4, "anointest" v. 5).

The word which is used in Psalm 23 to express these three ways in which God is active is "mercy" (v. 6). This word translates the Hebrew word *chesed*, which in other psalms is also translated "steadfast love", "kindness", "loving-kindness", and "love unfailing".

There are further truths about God's *chesed*:

1. It is especially for those who want to be loyal to God, i.e. for the people of Israel. See Psalm 103.18, "is upon those who keep His covenant".

2. It is shown to them even when they have disobeyed Him. So *chesed* is like the New Testament word "grace".

3. It is given because God has promised to give it.

4. It lasts for ever. See Psalm 103.17.

We see here an answer to the question, "How can people endure uncertainty?" It is through seeing that God is both active and "merciful".

## 3. THE RESPONSE

The worshippers responded to God with this psalm of confidence. They were not saying, "Do not worry: these things may never happen", but, "Even if great troubles are coming, we see that God is actively providing for us and for those for whom we are responsible. We do not know what the future holds, but we know who holds the future." This is "confidence" (or "trust" or "belief") in God. See note on "trust", p. 99.

Psalm 23 is in two parts:

**Vv. 1–4:** Confidence that God is a good shepherd.

**Vv. 5, 6:** Confidence that God is a good host.

## USE

Those who first used this psalm, used it as part of the worship which took place at the Temple in Jerusalem. The congregation, led by the priests, recognized God as active mainly because of the things which they knew that He had done in times past. God had done these things because of the "Covenant" or "special agreement" which He had made with the Israelites. In several passages in the Old Testament we see that writers used the words "shepherd and his flock" when they were thinking of this Covenant. See note on Psalm 103.18.

Some of the actions in this Temple worship may be actually referred to in this psalm. "Thou anointest my head with oil" (v. 5b) may mean that priests publicly anointed certain people of the congregation with oil, as a sign of the care that God had for them. "Thou preparest a table before me" (v. 5) may mean that, after the priests had offered a sacrifice, the people shared together some of the food. Again, this would be a sign that the people as a community were being cared for by God.

Christians have used this psalm more than any other psalm. Two of the many ways in which congregations have used it are the following:

(a) In a "metrical version", see General Note B, p. 118, e.g. the hymn which begins:

> The Lord's my shepherd, I'll not want,
> He makes me down to lie
> In pastures green; he leadeth me
> The quiet waters by.

There are also several other metrical versions in English, e.g. George Herbert's hymn, written about 1600, "The God of love my shepherd is"; Joseph Addison's hymn, "The Lord my pasture shall prepare"; and H. W. Baker's "The King of love my shepherd is".

(b) Many hymns have been written which are based on Psalm 23. See the Hindi hymn on p. 121.

(c) Many congregations sing it by the "sharing" method, see General Note B, p. 118. In France Joseph Gelineau chose v. 6a as the chorus, which was translated in English as "His goodness and mercy shall follow all the days of my life". (This can be obtained as a cassette from Grail.)

Many translators of Psalm 23 have used picture-language more suited to their own surroundings (for example, in countries where there are no sheep). One Japanese Christian who was an athlete was accustomed to running with a "pace-setter", that is, with a more experienced runner

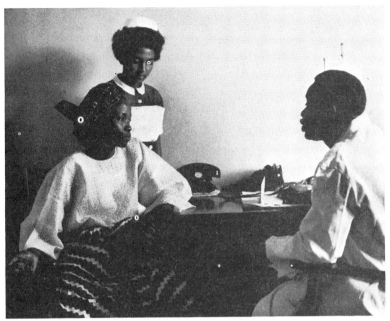

"The Lord is my shepherd" (Ps. 23.1).

To whose guidance can we today compare the guidance of God? This West African doctor's? This Russian policeman's?

who accompanies the runners on their training. He wrote a version which began

The Lord is my pace-setter, I shall not rush;
He makes me stop and rest for quiet intervals.
He provides me with images of stillness, which restore my serenity;
He leads me in ways of efficiency through calmness of mind,
And His guidance is peace.
Even though I have a great many things to accomplish each day,
I will not fret, for His presence is here . . .

## NOTES

**Ps. 23.1: My shepherd.** Why did the writer compare God to a shepherd? The answer becomes clear when we think what an Israelite shepherd's work was. He took the sheep out of the village to a place where there was grass for them to eat. Often he had to walk five or ten miles with them, over rocky dry ground, before he could find grass. He went in front of them to show the way and to protect them. It was dangerous work. In those days there were many wild animals in Palestine. When David was looking after sheep he had to fight a lion and a bear (1 Sam. 17.34, 35). The shepherd had to go on looking after his sheep in the heat of the day and throughout the very cold nights. His job was to bring them back safely to the village.

The Israelites had been keeping sheep for a long time, so it is not surprising that they called God "shepherd" and called themselves His "flock". "We are the sheep of his pasture" (Ps. 100); "He will feed his flock like a shepherd" (Isa. 40.11); "Thus says the Lord God, 'I myself will search for my sheep' " (Ezek. 34.11).

As we have seen, the Israelites believed that God was their shepherd in a special way because of the "Covenant" which He had made with them. They thought of this "Covenant" as a special agreement between God and the whole people of Israel (see note on Ps. 103.18). But since those days, worshippers both Jewish and Christian have come to see that God is also the shepherd of each single individual, so that each person can say, "*My* shepherd".

When Jesus Christ came He showed people more fully how God was their shepherd. God was in Christ, who was "The good shepherd who lays down his life for the sheep" (John 10.11). This shows us that the first worshippers were saying something even more important than they themselves knew. It does not mean that they knew (by magic or prediction) that Jesus would come. It means that they had seen a part of the truth about God, and this truth was fully seen when Jesus came. See note on Psalm 22.7.

**Ps. 23.3: Restores my soul.** These words are often translated "restores *me"* or "restores *my life"*, because God is concerned with the whole of a person. In neither the Old nor the New Testament do we read that part of a person called his soul can be separated from the rest of him, as if he had a lump inside him, which could be labelled "soul".

It is the "restoring" (rescuing, saving) of each of us (each as a whole person) that Christ was on earth to achieve, by His living and dying and rising. Through Christ it is possible for human beings to put away old ways of living. "You must be made new in mind and spirit, and put on the new nature" (Eph. 4.23).

It sometimes happens suddenly. In several parts of the world many young people are under the control of harmful drugs (heroin, cocaine, etc.). But groups of these "addicts", e.g. in Hong Kong, have accepted the power of the Holy Spirit, and have been set free from their addiction. Some of them have fallen back since that time, but others still say that God "restored" them at that time.

It sometimes happens gradually. Some Indian theologians, of whom Nehemiah Joreh of Benares was the first, have expressed the Christian Gospel in the language of Hinduism. Most of these theologians only became Christians after many years of prayer and thought and discussion.

And St Paul reminded readers that God offers this "restoring" many times during their lives: "Be renewed in the spirit of your minds" (Eph. 4.23). See note on p. 61.

In the RSV and some other translations we find "restores"; in other versions "shall restore". The reason for this is that it is not possible to tell from the Hebrew which is correct. (The same is true of verse 4, where some translations have "shall fear no evil", others "fear no evil"). But this is not a serious problem, because what God *has* done and *is* doing, He also *will* do. This is why, if we trust Him now, we can go on trusting Him in the future also. This same problem concerning the tense of verbs applies to the whole book of Psalms.

**Ps. 23.4a: Through the valley of the shadow.** A shepherd often had to lead his sheep through dark narrow places where sheep-stealers, or wild animals such as hyenas and jackals, might attack them. So God is present to give strength in the dark places of human beings' lives, in the pain and sadness of failure, in times of sin, danger, illness, loneliness, fear, doubt, and in death. The word "death" is not found in the Hebrew version of this psalm, but those who can trust God in other "dark places of life" can also trust Him in the time of death.

God does not promise to take believers out of these dark places, although in fact He sometimes does that. What He does promise is to give them strength while they are in such places. See note on Psalm 91.4.

The writer of Psalm 138 also makes this plain. Psalm 138 is probably a king's thanksgiving for victory, "I give thee thanks O Lord with my whole heart" (v. 1). Its plan is

Vv. 1–3: Thanks be to God.
Vv. 4–6: God will overcome evil.
Vv. 7, 8: God's steadfast love is with me in the midst of trouble.

According to 2 Corinthians 12.9 Paul discovered this in connection with a bodily complaint. He prayed that it should be taken away. When it was (apparently) not taken away, he accepted as God's answer "My grace is all you need". See also Philippians 4.13: "I have strength for anything through him who gives me power" (NEB).

**Ps. 23.4b: Thy rod and thy staff.** These two words are probably two names for one stick. This stick had a hook at one end (so that it is sometimes called a "crook"). Shepherds used, and still use, this kind of stick to drive away other animals, to prevent a sheep from going the wrong way, to pull up a sheep which has fallen into a hole in the rock, or to tap the hard ground at night to show the sheep where he, the shepherd, is. So it becomes a sign of the strength and comfort which God offers mankind.

**Ps. 23.6b: I shall dwell in the house of the Lord for ever.** By saying or singing these words the worshippers were again expressing their trust in God. Each was saying: "I believe that, in spite of so much uncertainty and danger, I shall never be separated from the fellowship of God, nor from the fellowship of others who worship at the Temple, 'the house of the Lord', as long as I live." We note that, for them, fellowship with God and fellowship with other worshippers went together. They needed to meet other worshippers in order to maintain their confidence in God.

We may note here similar words from Psalm 16.10, "Thou dost not give me up to Sheol or let thy chosen one see the pit". The writer of Psalm 16 was like the writer of Psalm 23: he asked for God's help, "Preserve me O God" (v. 1); and also expressed his confidence in God, "In thy presence there is fullness of joy" (v. 11). One of the things that the writer of Psalm 16 was sure about was this: God would save him from an early death. It is not likely that either he or the writer of Psalm 23 believed that they could have fellowship with God after death.

But Christians who use this psalm will want to say more than this.

First, to a Christian "for ever" will mean not simply "as long as I live", but "even after death". Before the coming of Christ it was not possible to say this. Paul wrote in Romans 8.38, 39: "I am sure that neither death, nor life . . . nor things present, nor things to come . . . will be able to separate us from the love of God", but he added that this is only true "in Christ Jesus our Lord".

Secondly, Christians have found that they can worship and serve God anywhere. The "house of the Lord" is not a church building, it is the world.

## STUDY SUGGESTIONS

WORDS

1. Psalm 23 is an act of "confidence" in God. Choose *three* out of the following phrases which have the same or nearly the same meaning as "confidence":
reliance on    understanding of    trust in    respect for
contemplation of    faith in.
2. In the RSV the Hebrew word *chesed* in Psalm 23.6 is translated "mercy". Compare this with:
(a) The translation of it given in another English version.
(b) The translation of it given in any other language you know, and say what other words in that language, if any, could be used instead.

CONTENT

3. Are the following statements true or untrue? Give reasons for your answer in each case:
(a) God delivers from suffering those who trust Him.
(b) The writer of Psalm 23 was sure there was life after death.
(c) The "house of the Lord" (Ps. 23.6) means the church building where we worship.
4. (a) What is the work of a shepherd?
(b) What makes it hard work?
(c) What does a shepherd use a "staff" for?

BIBLE

5. Read Psalm 138.
(a) In what two ways are Psalms 23 and 138 alike?
(b) Why do you think people have valued and used Psalm 23 even more than Psalm 138?
6. In Psalm 23.3 we read that God "restores" (RSV).
(a) Compare this translation with the words used in this verse in as many other modern English versions as you can.
(b) Which *three* of the following verses contain the same belief about God?
Ps. 24.8   Ps. 51.12   Isaiah 40.31   Rom. 12.2   Rom. 12.9
(c) Give the words used in the RSV to express this belief in each case.
7. Read Psalm 16.10
(a) What verse of Psalm 23 is this verse like?
(b) In what way are the two verses *un*like?

DISCUSSION AND RESEARCH

8. A probation officer, whose work is to help boys and girls who have broken the law of their country, once said, "Psalm 23 is fine for

43

little children, but not for us. 'I shall not want' (v. 1) is not true. Nor is verse 2, for God has not led me or the young people whom I look after 'beside still waters'." What would you reply to him?

9. (a) Why did the writer of Psalm 23 describe God as a "shepherd" and in what way were God's people the Israelites like sheep?

(b) Make a list of the things which you can picture in your mind as you read Psalm 23, e.g. a shepherd, a green pasture, etc.

(c) Which of these things are well known to everyone in the district where you live, and which are not?

(d) Re-write Psalm 23 along the lines of "The Lord is my pace-setter" (p. 40), so as to express your own experience and recognition of God. I.e. begin by substituting for "shepherd" some other person who gives you guidance and support today, and then change the rest of the psalm to fit.

10. "All these people were in situations of uncertainty and worry"· (p. 36)

(a) Give another example of such a situation.

(b) Make a list of all the possible things you might do if you were in that situation.

(c) What do you think would most help you to recognize God as "active and merciful"?

11. A leader or "minister" in the Church is sometimes called a "pastor", which is a Latin word meaning "shepherd". Describe:

(a) the ways in which a minister's work is *like* that of a shepherd,

(b) the ways in which it is unlike.

12. In Psalm 23.5 we read of "enemies".

(a) What would you mean by this word "enemies" if you used it in conversation?

(b) What difference, if any, is there between the attitude to enemies as expressed in Psalm 23.5, and the attitude expressed in the following passages?

Luke 6.27   Rom. 12.20   2 Thess. 3.15

(c) How far is it true to say that the more Christian we are the more enemies we shall have?

# General Note A
# The Psalms were for Temple Worship
# Example, Psalm 24

Most modern scholars think that the Israelites usually wrote psalms for Temple services. We may see more clearly what this means by studying one psalm in particular, taking as an example Psalm 24. As soon as we read verse 3 of this psalm, "Who shall ascend the hill of the Lord?", we see that the singers were taking part in a procession. They had come from many places to the city of Jerusalem to celebrate a festival. They had met at the foot of Mount Zion and were looking up at it. It was the same mountain or hill which David had captured, and on which Solomon had built the first Temple. A high wall surrounded it. As the singers marched, they rejoiced that in the beginning God had overcome disorder and established a world over which He has control. "The earth is the Lord's" (v. 1).

The musicians and singers led the procession. Next came those who carried the Ark. In the centre of the procession came the king, as God's own representative. A great crowd followed.

Then the procession halted, and one singer asked, "Who can climb God's hill?" (see v. 3). Another singer shouted the answer, "Those who have pure hearts" (see vv. 4, 5). Then the first singer said "Yes, those are the people who can find God in Temple worship" (see v. 6).

Then the procession went on up the long path that led to the Temple. When they reached the Temple gates, they found them shut. Then they sang (or shouted) like this:

First, a choir, or perhaps all the people, sang verse 7, "Lift up your heads, O gates!" i.e. "Let the gates be opened so that God can come in to give new life to His people and to the soil on which their lives depend."

Then a singer from inside the gates asked "Who is this God?" (see v. 8a). All the people answered "It is the mighty Lord . . ." (see v. 8b). Then they sang again, "Let the gates be opened" (see v. 9), and again a singer asked "Who is this God?" (see v. 10a). Then the people used God's great name, and shouted, "It is the Lord of Hosts" (see v. 10b).

When the people had used this name, the gates were opened and all went into the Temple to begin the festival. They offered a sacrifice, and they shared a meal, showing that they had a Covenant with God. It was for this that the worshippers had been preparing as they sang the psalm.

It is clear that the words of Psalm 24 were not written for private use. They belong to congregational worship. Very many other psalms are of this sort, e.g. some are *Lamentations* (see notes on pp. 52 and 70), and some are *Thanksgivings* (see notes on pp. 80 and 152). Most were *Festival Psalms*.

SOME WERE PSALMS FOR SPECIAL FESTIVALS

Very many psalms were used at the three great Israelite festivals:

(a) The spring festival in March or April. The Israelites used this festival to remember the "Passover" (how God had rescued them from Egypt), and also called it the Feast of Unleavened Bread.

(b) The mid-summer festival in June, which was a thanksgiving for the first fruits or grain of the year, i.e. the beginning of the harvest. It was called Feast of Weeks (and later "Pentecost").

(c) The autumn festival which went on during September and October, called "In-gathering", i.e. the end of the harvest. This was the most important of the three Festivals. Later the Israelites used it to commemorate their years of wandering in the wilderness, and called it the Feast of Booths or Tabernacles (i.e. tents).

Many scholars use other names for this autumn festival: "New Year Festival", "Covenant Festival", "God's Enthronement Festival", and believe that most of the psalms were written with these themes in mind and for this festival. The title "Covenant Festival" is used because the Israelites renewed the Covenant which God had made with them. The title "Enthronement Festival" is used because the worshippers accepted God as their king for a new year.

Although writers in the Bible do not use these titles, they do refer to "The Feast", e.g. Zechariah 14.16 and Numbers 29.12–38.

Each festival had its own special purpose. But there were some things which were done at all of them, and the psalms were written to help the worshippers to do these things e.g.:

(a) The people *remembered what God had done in the past*, especially that he rescued them from Egypt, that He had appeared to Moses on Mount Sinai (Exod. 24.15–18), and that He had made a special agreement or "Covenant" with them (Exod. 24.3–8).

(b) The people's singing and other worship was their *response* to what God had done for them.

(c) They made their response by *reading and reciting* the stories of what God had done and *acting out* these stories in drama. See note on symbolic worship, p. 47.

(d) They met in order to *renew their Covenant* with God. But this could not be done by those who were worshipping other "gods" (which were not really gods), or who were living in disobedience to God. So the Israelites often used a preparation like that in vv. 3–6 of Psalm 24.

(e) Each time that the people remembered the actions of God, *they remembered that He was with them* and that He was saving them and strengthening them. Thus they could say that in the temple they were "receiving blessing and salvation" (Ps. 24.5).

(f) So they went home after the service, *ready to obey God* in their homes and farms and market-places.

## SOME WERE "HYMNS" AND "ROYAL PSALMS"

Two sorts of psalm were used more than others at these festivals:

(a) *Hymns* is the name which most scholars give to those psalms in which the worshippers praised God and gave the reasons why they praised Him. "Rejoice in the Lord . . . For the word of the Lord is upright" (Ps. 33.1, 4). Note that the word "hymn" is used in two different ways: these "Hymns" are different from the hymns of various sorts which most Christian congregations sing today.

The theme of some of the psalms called "Hymns" is the "enthronement" of God, e.g. the worshippers renew their belief that God is supreme King in the world. See note on p. 109.

The theme of other "Hymns" is Zion (Jerusalem), i.e. that it was in Zion that God made Himself known to His people. Psalm 24 is one of these psalms.

(b) *Royal Psalms* have as their theme the Israelite king. The worshippers prayed for him on special occasions, e.g. when he was enthroned, or married, or going into battle. They regarded their king as God's own representative, and therefore when they prayed for their king's success they were also praying that God Himself should be honoured and obeyed. See note on Psalm 72.8.

## Symbolic Worship

In the Psalms themselves we read of many different actions which the worshippers performed during worship, and which were a help to them as they worshipped. (We have already noted some in studying Psalm 24.) It is true that such actions could actually prevent the Israelites from worshipping God in their hearts, and that the prophets pointed this out ("I take no delight in your solemn assemblies", Amos 5.21). But in general the worshippers found such actions to be a help rather than a hindrance.

The following are some of the chief actions referred to in the Psalms:

(a) The worshippers marched in procession: "The solemn processions are seen" (Ps. 68.24).

(b) They carried the ark: "Arise, O Lord . . . thou and the ark of thy might" (Ps. 132.8).

(c) They danced: "Praise his name with dancing" (Ps. 149.3).

(d) They sacrificed animals and birds: "May he regard with favour your burnt sacrifices!" (Ps. 20.3).

(e) They burned incense: "Let my prayer be counted as incense before thee" (Ps. 141.2).

(f) They prostrated themselves on the ground, or knelt: "Let us worship and bow down, let us kneel before the Lord" (Ps. 95.6).

(g) They washed themselves: "I wash my hands" (Ps. 26.6).

(h) They clapped their hands: "Clap your hands" (Ps. 47.1).

(i) They shouted and sang: "Shout to God" (Ps. 47.1).

(j) They drank from a cup: "I will lift up the cup of salvation" (Ps. 116.13).

(k) They ate a meal together: "Thou preparest a table before me" (Ps. 23.5).

(l) They played musical instruments, see General Note B, p. 117.

We should also note the words and phrases which refer to other things which the worshippers did or saw as they used the Psalms. Many of these words, such as "face", "beauty", "presence", refer to the wooden "mercy-seat" on the Ark in the Holy of Holies in the Temple, and to the two wings of the carved cherubim on the mercy-seat, for example: "Seek the *face* of God" (Ps. 24.6), "Behold the *beauty* of the Lord" (Ps. 27.4), "Come into his *presence*" (Ps. 95.2). The worshippers did not think that the wings were God. But as they looked at the wings they remembered that God was present with them in all His power. See also notes on Psalms 42.2 and 139.7b.

There are many things that we do not know concerning the way in which the Israelites used the Psalms. We do not know when or why each psalm was written, nor on what occasions each psalm was used. But it is certain that the Israelites used most of them at public Temple services. We can only understand the Psalms if we remember this.

# Further comment on Psalm 24

## THEME

Psalm 24 is in three parts:

**Vv. 1, 2:** We praise you, Lord, because you are the giver and controller of all life.

**Vv. 3–6:** We realize that we must honour you in daily life as well as in public worship.

**Vv. 7–10:** We praise you again because you have always been "mighty in battles" against the disorders of the world.

## USE

A good way in which a congregation today can say or sing this psalm is as follows:

Congregation:     Alleluia, Alleluia, Alleluia
Leader or Singer: Verses 1 and 2
Congregation:     Alleluia (3 times, as above)
Leader:           vv. 3, 4
Congregation:     Alleluia (as above)
Leader:           vv. 5, 6
Congregation:     Alleluia (as above)
Leader:           v. 7

"Actions which the worshippers performed were a help to them" (p. 47).

People of nearly all religions use symbolic actions in their worship. A Hindu in Sri Lanka makes an offering as part of his worship of a god. A Church leader in Central Africa exchanges the "kiss of peace" with a member of his congregation.

When are such actions a help and when are they a hindrance?

49

Half congregation:     Who is the King of Glory:
The other half:     The Lord of hosts, He is the King of Glory.

The leader then says or sings verses 8, 9, 10 and after each verse the two halves of the congregation repeat their chorus "Who is . . . ?"
See a Luganda version of Psalm 24 on p. 122.

## NOTES

**Ps. 24.3, 4: Who shall ascend . . . ? . . . He who has clean hands . . .**
In v. 1 the writer was saying, "God set all things in order when He created the world, and He is the controller of all life. He made life and offers it to us." Then in vv. 3–6 he says, "But we cannot fully share in the life God offers us unless we live in the way which He has planned." Compare Psalm 15.

Psalm 15 is like Psalm 24 in two ways. First, it was probably used by those who marched in procession to the Temple. Secondly, it concerns the way people live, i.e. it contains instructions for learners. See note on Psalm 19.7, numbered paragraph 3. Both Psalm 24.3, 4 and Psalm 15.1, 2 contain the same question and answer:
Q: Who can worship God fully at public services?
A: Those who do their best to serve Him in their daily lives.

This is the sort of teaching about behaviour which the Israelite prophets also gave. And they used to add, "There is something wrong with your worship unless it helps you to be loyal to God and to your fellow human-beings, to care for your old parents, and to do a full day's work in return for your wages when you leave Temple worship." "Take away from me the noise of your songs . . . let justice roll down like waters" (Amos 5.23, 24).

**Ps. 24.6: Such is the generation of those who seek him.** The Jerusalem Bible translation is better, "Such are the *people* who seek him", i.e. such is the procession of people who are worshipping Him.

**Ps. 24.6, 10: Selah.** Thirty-nine psalms contain this word, but no one knows its meaning. Probably it is a direction to the musicians and singers, "Play your instruments at this point" or "Shout here!".

**Ps. 24.7, 9: That the king of glory may come in.** The worshippers knew that God does not really have to come. As they sang He was already present. But these words were their way of saying that they needed (a) to be *ready* for Him, and (b) to *remember* that He was present. See John 14.23. "If a man loves me . . . my Father will love him and we will come to him."

## STUDY SUGGESTIONS

CONTENT

1. What *two* reasons are there for thinking that the Israelites used Psalm 24 as they marched in procession to the Temple?

2. (a) By what *two* names did the Israelites usually call the great festival which they celebrated in September and October?
   (b) Why was each of these names used?
3. (i) Give one example of an action which Israelites sometimes performed during their worship.
   (ii) What did that action symbolize, i.e. what was its meaning?
   (iii) What symbolic actions do we read about in the following passages:
   (a) Ps. 27.6  (b) Ps. 150.4  (c) 1 Kgs. 8.4, 5  (d) 2 Chron. 29.27–29

BIBLE

4. In what way are verses 3–6 of Psalm 24 like (a) Psalm 15, (b) Matthew 5.8?
5. (a) How is the phrase "does not swear deceitfully" (Ps. 24.4c) translated in (i) another English version, (ii) another language version?
   (b) Give an example from everyday life of someone who "does not swear deceitfully".

DISCUSSION AND RESEARCH

6. Do you think that you could use Psalm 24 in an act of Christian worship?
   (a) If so, what could you say or do as leader to help the congregation to make it their worship of God?
   (b) If not, give your reasons.
7. (a) In what hymns or written prayers, or at what other times, in your Church do you ask God to "come"?
   (b) What would you reply to someone who said that asking God to "come in" is meaningless because He is always present?

# The Flowing Stream
## Psalms 42 and 43

## THEME

### 1. THE EXPERIENCE: LONELINESS

A person can be happy when alone, but not happy when lonely. All Christians need to be alone sometimes, to learn how to live with themselves in the presence of God, to experience silence in solitude, to experience death. But this is not the same as being "lonely". It is possible for people to feel very lonely even when they are in a crowded street or living in a big family.

Most people feel the pain of loneliness because they have lost the people or the things which had supported them. A woman marries a man from another race and is no longer among her own people. A widow feels the loss of the husband on whom she depended. Very old people have very few friends of their own age. People who become blind and deaf remember the time when they could communicate freely with others. People in great physical pain feel that they are cut off from those around them. A leader who must take decisions on his own, wishes that he could still share his responsibilities with others. Very brave people who have acted against custom have become unpopular, or they have been imprisoned, and long for the freedom they once enjoyed.

The Israelite who first made these two psalms as his prayer to God had had the sort of experience described above. We do not know if he was alone or whether there were others with him. Nor do we know if he had been taken into exile, e.g. into Syria, or if he was a soldier with an army a long way from home. But he certainly felt the pain of losing something that had supported him. In his case this was Temple worship. It was at Temple services that he had received strength from God and had accepted responsibility for carrying out God's demands. He remembered how he used to go "with the throng and led them in procession to the house of God" (Ps. 42.4). Now, instead of receiving that support, he was living among "unbelievers" who laughed at his beliefs (Pss. 42.3 and 42.10).

## 2. THE RECOGNITION OF GOD

Somehow this lonely Israelite was able to see beyond his loneliness to God. In spite of his feeling of being separated from God, he could still reach out to Him and pray to Him.

The phrases and words which he used in referring to God show what he believed about God. We may note three in particular:

1. "Steadfast love" (Ps. 42.8). See note on p. 37.

2. "Rock" (Ps. 42.9). God was like a firm rock in the middle of a river which was difficult to cross because of its waves and billows (Ps. 42.7); He was like a rock which gives shade to travellers in the desert; like a rock from which a man could protect himself against an enemy; like a rock which stands firm when the wind blows everything else away. The Israelites often used this word to express their trust in God as their defender and sustainer.

3. "Truth" (Ps. 43.3). We usually think of "truth" as the opposite of a lie. But when the Israelites called God "true" they meant chiefly that He was trustworthy, reliable, and consistent. The Hebrew word is *emeth*, and is also translated "faithfulness". God kept His Covenant with His people. He kept His promises. He continued to care for them even when they forgot Him. We often find the word in the phrase "God's

mercy and truth" as in Psalm 25.10 (RSV "God's steadfast love and faithfulness").

## 3. THE RESPONSE

The worshipper's response to God, the steadfastly loving, the rock, the truth, was the single prayer which we have as the two Psalms 42 and 43. In this prayer:

(a) The worshipper showed his dependence on God, "My soul thirsts for God" (Ps. 42.2.). He needed to find God as much as a deer or a mountain goat needs to find water in the dry season when most of the rivers and pools are empty.

(b) He made his request to God. He asked for two things:

(i) Protection against the people he was living among, those who said "Your God is too weak to save you? What is the use of such a God?" "Where is your God?" (Ps. 42.3). "Defend my cause" (Ps. 43.1).

(ii) An early return to the Temple worship "Send out thy light and thy truth . . . let them bring me to thy holy hill" (Ps. 43.3.)

See the note on pp. 57 and 58 about prayers of request.

(c) He complained to God, "Why hast thou forgotten me?" (Ps. 42.9). Here, as in Psalm 22, the worshipper openly places before God his perplexity and his anger. We could compare his feelings with those of a Zambian student who had been sent out to do his teaching-practice in a faraway village school. He found that there was no equipment and complained bitterly to his college staff that they had left him without help.

See the note on pp. 29 and 30 about prayers of complaint.

(d) He expressed his hope in God. He had enough confidence in God to believe that He could somehow answer his prayer. See the chorus verse (Ps. 42.5).

But this worshipper only reached this hope-in-God through a struggle with himself. We may see this struggle in verses such as the following:

It is very hard to have faith in God (Ps. 42.3).
But I trust Him (Ps. 42.5b).
He seems to have forgotten me (Ps. 42.9).
But I belong to Him (Ps. 42.11).

The plan of this response (which covers both Psalms 42 and 43) is as follows:

**42.1–4:**  First strophe—A prayer of longing for God.
**42.5a:**  Chorus—Hope in God.
**42.5b–10:**  Second strophe—The prayer continued.
**42.11:**  Chorus.
**43.1–4:**  Third strophe—A request for help.
**43.5:**  Chorus.

"I say to God . . . why hast thou forgotten me?" (Ps. 42.9).

What can give hope to a lonely person—a person like this old Algerian woman who is being moved from her home, for political reasons, to a part of the country where she has no friends?

## USE

1. As we have seen, this psalm was probably first used as a prayer uttered in exile. Later it became part of the regular public worship of the Israelites. It was an appeal for help in all times of special need, and an expression of every human being's search for God.

2. One special way in which Christians have used it is as a preparation for Holy Communion. This is chiefly because of Psalm 43.4: "I will go to the altar of God".

3. In congregational use it is good to sing the chorus verse as a chorus. See also General Note B, p. 122, for one way in which this can be done.

On the other hand, congregations may use the "Metrical Psalm", written 300 years ago (see General Note B, p. 116), which is printed in many hymnbooks. It uses Psalm 42.1, 2, 9 and 11 only. Its first verse is:

> As pants the hart for cooling streams,
> When heated in the chase,
> So longs my soul, O God, for Thee,
> And thy refreshing grace.

## NOTES

**Ps. 42.1 and 7: Flowing streams . . . thy waves and billows.** For the writer, in v. 1, water stands for the refreshment and life which God gives. But in v. 7, water represents a frightening wave in which a man could easily be drowned; it is a danger from which he asks God to rescue him. See note on Psalm 130.1.

These two verses show two of the chief ways in which writers throughout the Bible think of water. And there is a third way: water is also the thing which makes clean, or the sign that God has forgiven a man. See note on Psalm 51.2.

**Ps. 42.2: Behold the face of God.** This is one of the phrases used in these two psalms which refer to the things which worshippers saw and did in the services of the Temple. "To behold God's face" meant to be present in the congregation as the Ark of the Covenant was carried in. As worshippers saw the Ark they were aware of God's presence. They were "before His face"; they were "beholding" it. See General Note A, p. 48. Similar phrases in this psalm are:

| | |
|---|---|
| "led them in procession" (Ps. 42.4) | danced or marched into the Temple. |
| "glad shouts and songs" (Ps. 42.4) | the Psalms. |
| "holy hill" (Ps. 43.3) | Mount Zion on which was the Temple. |

"thy dwelling" (Ps. 43.3)      the Temple.

"the altar of God" (Ps. 43.4)      the place where sacrifices of animals were offered.

"the lyre" (Ps. 43.4)      one of the instruments used to accompany the singing. See note on p. 117.

It was this kind of activity which the writer of this psalm was longing to share once again. See General Note A, p. 47.

We may note three other psalms (27, 84, and 122) in which the writers show how important the Temple (and Jerusalem) was to them.

Psalm 27 ("The Lord is my light and my salvation: whom shall I fear?") is a prayer of confidence in God (vv. 1–6 and vv. 13, 14) and is also a cry for help (vv. 7–12). The writer prays confidently (v. 4): "That I may dwell in the house of the Lord".

Psalm 84 is one of the "Hymns of Zion". See General Note A, p. 47. Pilgrims who were travelling to the Temple at the Feast of Tabernacles may have sung it. It is in three parts:

Vv. 1–4: The happiness or "blessedness' of those who worship at the Temple (especially v. 4).

Vv. 5–9: The happiness of the pilgrims.

Vv. 10–12: The happiness of worshippers at the Temple who in their daily lives trust God.

Psalm 122 is another "Hymn of Zion". Its plan is:

Vv. 1, 2: The joy of congregational worship at the Temple: "I was glad . . ." (v. 1).

Vv. 3–5: Jerusalem and its Temple are a centre to which all Israelites go, and which therefore provides unity.

Vv. 6–9: May Jerusalem have "peace"! See note on Psalm 72.7.

**Ps. 42.4: I went with the throng.** The writer found it very difficult to keep his faith in God without being an active member of a worshipping congregation. Indeed, it was only because he had been brought up to worship God in this way that he was able to pray to God at all when he was in exile. Is this true for Christians? Is it necessary for Christians to attend public worship regularly? The following points may help us to answer these questions:

1. The people who are the Church are Christ's body (1. Cor. 12.27), i.e. people through whom Christ works in the world. Christians need to commit themselves to membership of some Christian group in order that they may join in serving God's human family. See p. 30. It may meet anywhere: in a church or a schoolroom, in somebody's house or under a tree.

2. This group is called on by God also to meet the needs of its members. This does not happen in every Church. A man and a woman came to the minister of a church in the town where the woman lived,

and asked to be married in that church. The man said he did not go to Church in his village. The minister said, "But when you have made your marriage vows, you will need the help which people receive from belonging to a Church congregation". The man said, "Don't you know my village? The Church people there are a group who keep themselves apart; they are the last people in the village from whom anyone could expect help". And the minister knew that this was true.

3. A congregation becomes strong and effective when it has in it members who have a personal belief in God. Such people have learnt two things:

(a) How to join in a congregation;

(b) How to do without it when it is impossible to have it.

4. God is at work in other places besides the church building. In people's homes and in the places where people meet and work, God gives them strength and calls on them to serve Him.

**Ps. 42.5: Hope in God.** In English we often misuse the word "hope". We confuse it with "optimism". Or we say "I hope it will rain soon" when we really mean "I want it to rain soon".

For writers in the Bible a person who "hopes", hopes in God. He is willing to wait without anxiety because he knows something about God's character. He has faith in God as regards the future. So when Jesus came, His followers felt that they had even more reason to hope, because they had discovered more about God. *"Through him* you have confidence in God who raised him from the dead . . . so that your faith and hope are in God" (1 Pet. 1.21).

Martin Luther King, the Christian Civil Rights leader in the USA, had this kind of hope. In one of his famous speeches he said: "I have a dream that one day on the red hills of Georgia the sons of former slaves and the sons of former slave-owners will be able to sit down together at the table of brotherhood . . . I have a dream that my four little children will one day live in a nation where they will not be judged by the colour of their skins, but by the content of their character. I have a dream today."

**Ps. 42.6: the land of Jordan and of Hermon.** These words probably show that the writer had been exiled to some place near the source of the River Jordan, to the south-west of Mount Hermon.

**Ps. 43.1: defend my cause.** It is clear from these words that this psalm is partly a prayer of asking. Very many psalms are prayers of this kind, and a third of all the Psalms are requests in time of trouble.

Sometimes we can see what the worshipper was asking for: e.g. heal me (see Ps. 6.2), show me what I ought to do (see Ps. 25.4), give us victory in this war (see Ps. 60.5), give me strength in my old age (see Ps. 71.9), give me strength in my temptations (see Ps. 141.4).

Sometimes the request is general, and the writer does not say exactly what he is asking for. This is usually more suitable in public worship, or when prayers are being offered for the whole nation. But of course individual worshippers would use the general request to include their own special needs. See note on Psalm 116.1b.

As Christians also offer prayers of asking, the following notes may be added:

1. If an asking prayer is what we most want to offer to God, then it is good to offer it. We can be open and free in our approach to Him. Jesus said, "Ask . . . seek . . . knock" (Matt. 7.7).

2. We are sons of God, not his infants. When we ask God for something, we also dedicate ourselves to do everything possible ourselves to obtain it. "Work . . . for God is at work in you" (Phil. 2.12, 13).

3. We only know a little about what is best for us and for those around us. Since God does completely know what is best, the best prayer is "Thy will be done" (Matt. 6.10).

4. Asking is only part of prayer. Prayer itself is the placing of our whole personality and our whole existence in the presence of the loving and active God.

5. God is already giving us what we most need, even before we begin to ask. (See Isa. 65.24.)

## STUDY SUGGESTIONS

### WORDS

1. What did the Israelites mean when they called God "true"? Give one English word to explain this meaning, and one word in another language which you know.

### CONTENT

2. Make a list of the phrases and words which the writer of Psalms 42 and 43 used in addressing God.
3. What did the writer of Psalms 42 and 43 want more than anything else?
4. Which is the chorus in these two psalms?
5. The writer of Psalm 42 thinks of water in two very different ways. What are these two ways?

### BIBLE

6. "God, my rock" (Ps. 42.9). The writers of the following passages also compare God to a rock. Say in each case what special truth about God the writer had in mind.
   (a) Deut. 32.4  (b) Ps. 18.2  (c) Isa. 32.2
7. In the AV the Hebrew word *yachal* is usually translated "hope" in

the Psalms, and the Greek word *elpis* is usually translated "hope" in the New Testament.

In the following verses what word is used to translate these words in (i) the RSV; (ii) another language known to you:
(a) Ps. 31.24   (b) Ps. 38.15   (c) Ps. 130.7   (d) 1 Tim. 5.5

8. Read 2 Corinthians 5.6–9. In what way is this passage like Psalm 42 and 43?

9. In each of the following psalms the writers use phrases which "show how important the Temple (in Jerusalem) was to them" (p. 56). What are these phrases in each case?
(a) Ps. 27   (b) Pss 42 and 43   (c) Ps. 84   (d) Ps. 122

DISCUSSION AND RESEARCH

10. Give examples from everyday life to show the difference between "loneliness' and "being alone".

11. Give two examples of people, one from the past and one from the present day, who have been brave in acting against custom (p. 52). In each case say what custom they defied, and what the result was.

12. Draw a rough map of the country in which the writer of Psalms 42 and 43 lived, and mark on it:
Mount Hermon   the River Jordan   Jerusalem

13. "Is it necessary for Christians to attend public worship regularly?" (p. 56). What is your opinion? Give reasons for your answer.

14. What would you reply to someone who said: "It is impossible for God, who is the Creator and Sustainer of the whole universe, to be concerned with the details of my life. Asking is not part of my prayer."?

15. The writer reached his hope in God "through a struggle with himself" (p. 53). Write out as many verses or parts of verses from Psalms 42 and 43 as you can, so as to construct more fully the "struggle" or "conversation" which the writer was having with himself.

# The Open Lips
## Psalm 51

### THEME

#### 1. THE EXPERIENCE: PERSONAL GUILT

When someone has the experience of feeling guilty, he simply feels that there is a gap "between what I am and what I could be" or "between what I did and what I could have done".

It is useful to distinguish between three sorts of guilt-feeling:

1. False guilt, i.e. when we feel guilty although there is no real reason to feel guilty. We may feel we ought to have done something although in fact it was not possible for us to do it. A boy worked hard at school but failed to get the high marks in the final examination which his parents had expected him to get. He felt guilty because his parents were clearly disappointed and annoyed. Another child, a girl, overheard her father say to her mother "If only this one had been a boy!" This made her feel that because she was a girl she ought not really to be alive at all, and the feeling of guilt continued even when she was a grown up woman.

Although we call this feeling "false guilt", the feeling is just as painful as the feeling of real guilt.

2. Guilt for particular acts of wrong-doing, or for failure to do what ought to be done. We have this whether others regard the act as a "small" sin (a student makes an unkind and unfair remark about a fellow student in the latter's absence) or whether they regard it as a "serious" sin (a retired cashier is the treasurer of a co-operative society and secretly borrows its money to buy a house for himself).

3. Guilt for not being a better person, i.e. concerning the quality of one's life. A man looks at his son and knows that if he himself were a more courageous and honest and generous person he would be giving his son a better start in life than he is giving him. This father is not thinking of particular incidents. He is understanding himself and being aware of his own weakness.

So painful is this feeling of personal guilt that human beings try all sorts of unsuccessful ways of dealing with it. Here are some of those ways.

(a) They turn their attention to someone else's failings. Jesus talked about a carpenter who pointed to the speck of sawdust in his brother's eye but not to the plank of wood in his own! (Matt. 7.3). If a person notices that one of his neighbours shows some of the same weakness which he secretly knows is in himself, then he becomes angry, because the neighbour reminds him of something he wants to forget.

(b) They push the feeling out of sight. For many years a boy had one teacher who was cruelly severe, and made the boy feel guilty most of the time. The boy could not endure this, and so (without knowing that he was doing it) pushed all feelings of guilt out of his mind. He grew up quite unable to see that he was ever at fault. When he married, his wife found that he was a very difficult person to live with.

(c) They apologize a great deal for their many little mistakes in order not to think about their very large feeling of unworthiness.

(d) They overwork, sometimes to the point of collapse, as if they could in this way make amends for their sinfulness.

(e) They admit to making mistakes but believe that it is due to some weakness inherited from their parents or to the way their parents brought them up. They believe that they themselves are not responsible.

(f) They believe that they are completely evil and that there is nothing that they can do about it.

The above are examples of the sort of thing that people do in the hope of overcoming the pain of feeling guilty. But from these examples it is clear that, as a result of these actions, their condition becomes worse, not better

The writer of Psalm 51 had experienced the same painful feeling of guilt which we have already considered. He felt unclean ("wash me . . . cleanse me", v. 2). He asked to be renewed in every part of his life ("Put a new . . . spirit within me", v. 10). He could not put things right himself ("thou has no delight in sacrifice", v. 16).

How did he deal with this pain?

The answer is that he recognized that it was God Himself against whom he had done wrong, and that it was therefore God who could rescue him.

## 2. THE RECOGNITION OF GOD

First he recognized the *presence* of God. He saw that whatever sort of life he led, he led it in God's presence; and whatever he did, he did towards God. As St Paul said "If we live, we live to the Lord" (Rom. 14.8). So when he did wrong he wrote "Against thee, thee only, have I sinned" (Ps. 51.4). Some people can see that their sins harm other people. Some see that they are spoiling themselves when they sin. But this writer made the same discovery which St Paul made on his way to Damascus, when he knew that God was saying to him "Why do you persecute *me*?" (Acts 9.4). See note 2 on p. 167.

Secondly, he saw that God Himself was his *judge*: "Thou art . . . blameless in thy judgment" (Ps. 51.4).

At first sight we might expect the writer to feel more guilty, not less, in the presence of a judge. And no doubt that is just what he did feel. But he saw further than this.

He saw thirdly that God the stern judge was also God the *restorer*. Again St Paul seems to have shared this writer's experience: "God has consigned all men to disobedience, that he may have mercy upon all. O the depth of the riches and wisdom and knowledge of God!" (Rom. 11.32, 33).

The words and phrases from which we see that God "restores" are the following:

(a) "Create in me a clean heart" (v. 10a). The guilty person cannot himself do all that needs to be done in order to get rid of his guilt. He needs God to "create" him, or to "re-create" him. (The Hebrew word here translated "create" is the same as the word used in Genesis 1.1.)

(b) "A new and right spirit" (v. 10b) and "holy Spirit" (v. 11b). By referring to God's "spirit", the writer was saying that God gives Himself to human beings to create and re-create them. See notes on Psalms 23.3 and 51.11.

(c) "Thy steadfast love . . . thy abundant mercy" (v. 1). The writer knew that God does not treat a person according to that person's behaviour. The writer has not told us how he knew that God was like this. God forgives (but the writer of Psalm 51 does not use the word "forgive". See notes on Psalms 103.3a and 130.4a). How did the writer know that God was like this? Hosea knew through his own love for his wife that God is merciful. "The Lord said to me, 'Go again, love a woman who is . . . an adulteress; even as the Lord loves the people of Israel, though they turn to other gods' " (Hos. 3.1).

The writer was able to face the seriousness of his own sin and the painfulness of his strong feelings of guilt only because he had been able to recognize God as One who was actively concerned to rescue him. See note on Psalm 23.3.

## 3. THE RESPONSE

The writer's response to the "mercy" of God is this Psalm 51. People sometimes call it a "Prayer of Confession", but the following notes may show that it is much more than that. In many ways it helps to explain what "prayer" itself is.

(a) The writer faced the truth about himself in the presence of God, even truth that was painful, "I know my transgressions" (v. 3).

(b) He openly expressed his feelings to God. He did not use the words "Open thou my lips" till v. 15, but he had already done this himself from v. 1 onward. That is why we have used these words as title for this chapter.

(c) He gave himself time to see what God was like, "thy abundant mercy" (v. 1).

(d) He expressed his dependence upon God with common sense, "Create in me . . ." (v. 10).

(e) He offered himself to God, to be used by God: "I will teach . . ." (v. 13); "My mouth shall show forth thy praise" (v. 15).

The plan of Psalm 51 is as follows:

**Vv. 1–6:** A cry to the merciful God from one who recognizes his own sinfulness.

**Vv. 7–13:** A request to God for His forgiveness (vv. 7–9), and for His renewing power (vv. 10–13).

**Vv. 14–17:** A self-dedication by the worshipper.

**Vv. 18, 19:** These two verses were probably added by a later editor. See note on p. 67.

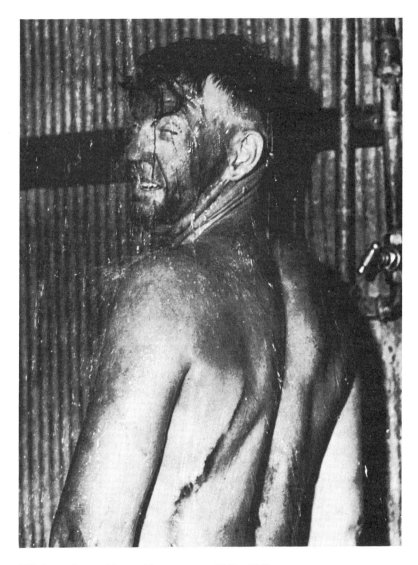

"Wash me thoroughly . . . Cleanse me . . .!" (Ps. 51.2).

God has provided the water which washes the coal dust from an Australian miner.
What has He provided to cleanse him in spirit?

## USE

1. When people first used Psalm 51 as part of the Temple worship, they probably performed dramatic and symbolic actions as they said or sang it. This seems likely from the following phrases:

"Cleanse" (v. 2): It was customary to pour water over a worshipper as a sign that God was forgiving him.

"Purge with hyssop" (v. 7): Another Israelite custom was to dip twigs of the hyssop plant in water and to sprinkle people who had been in touch with a leper (Lev. 14.4) or with a corpse (Num. 19.18).

"Presence" (v. 11): See General Note A, p. 48.

As we have seen, the Israelites found that when their leader performed such symbolic outward actions, they themselves were strengthened in their loyalty to God.

2. Christians have used this psalm (and Psalm 23) more than any other psalm. When it is sung with a chorus verse, v. 10 is obviously suitable:

> "Create in me a clean heart, O God,
> And put a new and right spirit within me."

It is used as a corporate prayer, e.g. on Ash Wednesday when many Churches use it. It also provides many verses which can become "arrow prayers", that is, short exclamations which can be made to God at any time of day or night.

*Note:* Psalm 51 and Psalm 130 may both have been personal prayers at one time, and almost certainly both became part of the corporate worship of the Temple at a later date. In this "Guide" we are regarding Psalm 51 chiefly as a personal prayer, arising from a feeling of personal guilt. We are treating Psalm 130 as a corporate prayer, arising from a feeling of corporate guilt. See pp. 156 to 158.

## NOTES

**Ps. 51.1: Thy abundant mercy.** The Hebrew word here translated "mercy" is *rachamaim*, one of two words which the writer uses to refer to God's kindness. The other word is *chesed* or "steadfast love". See note on p. 37.

*Rachamaim* is probably connected with the Hebrew word for a womb. It is as if the writer was speaking of the "mother love" of God. The special gifts and feelings which mothers have help us to understand the love of God just as much as the special gifts of fathers. Although it is convenient to refer to God as "He" and "Father", it is good to remember that He is not more masculine than He is feminine. Indeed, all such words about God are only picture-words. See notes on Psalms 96.10 and 103.13.

**Ps. 51.2: My sin.**

1. When David was Commander-in-chief of the Israelites, he sent Uriah, an officer of his army, to fight in a place where he would probably be killed. David did this because he wanted to marry Uriah's wife (2 Sam. 11 and 12), and later he felt deeply guilty. Many readers have suggested that David may have written Psalm 51 shortly after this incident. This interpretation may, of course, be a true one. On the other hand the writer does not seem to be referring so much to one single deed as to his whole sinfulness.

2. What was this "sinfulness" which made the writer feel guilty?

Three Hebrew words which the writer uses help to answer this question. They are here translated as:

"Transgressions": leaving those who are loyal to God and joining those who are in rebellion.

"Sin": failing to do what we mean to do or missing a target. This is the word used in Judges 20.16.

"Iniquity": being crooked, like a bent knife which the owner cannot use until it is mended.

Today we most often use the English word "sin" to describe the "sinfulness" which makes us feel guilty. But as people often misuse the word "sin", it is useful to notice other words which have a different meaning:

"Crime": a word used when someone breaks a law of his country,

"Shame": the bad feeling we have when other people find out that we have done wrong. (It has other meanings too.)

"Sins": actions which we commit because of our sin.

"Guilt": the feeling that results from being sinful.

"Sin" is different from these because it is a condition we are in, like being in bad health. This condition spoils our relationship with God, with other people, and with ourselves.

**Ps. 51.5: In sin did my mother conceive me.** The meaning is that sinfulness had been part of the writer's life for so long that he could not deal with it without God's help. Just as the air which he breathed as soon as he was born was in some ways impure, so as soon as he became a member of the human race he shared its sinfulness.

Readers of this psalm have sometimes interpreted these words wrongly, saying for instance:

(a) that the writer inherited sinfulness from his ancestors;

(b) that his mother committed sin by having the sexual intercourse which led to his being conceived, and that in this way she infected her son with evil.

But sex is one of the gifts from God, the Creator, and He means us to use it and to use it responsibly. It is only when people (including Christians) forget this truth that they make interpretations such as those referred to above.

**Ps. 51.8: The bones which thou hast broken.**
  1. Some people say that "broken bones" is only picture-language which the writer uses to describe the pain of his guilt.
  2. Others think that the writer was actually ill, and that he believed that God had sent him the illness as a punishment for sin (*"Thou* hast broken . . .").

The second of these views may well be the right one, and it is useful to notice the connection which writers in the Old Testament made between sin and illness. See notes on Psalms 22.15c and 91.8.

**Ps. 51.11: Thy Holy Spirit.** The Hebrew word here translated "Spirit" is *ruach*.

  (a) As this word means breath or wind, writers in the Old Testament sometimes thought of God's *ruach* as something that He keeps with him and which He sends out, e.g. to give life to a new baby.

  (b) Other writers used "spirit" to mean God Himself in action, not something that He sends, e.g. Genesis 1.2.

  (c) Later writers thought of God's spirit as God Himself as He meets human beings and "inspires" them. The results of this meeting are that people become strong leaders (Judg. 6.34), or become wise (Gen. 41.38), or become prophets (Isa. 61.1), or (as in this psalm) receive forgiveness and renewal.

**Ps. 51.16: Thou hast no delight in sacrifice.** It is unlikely that this writer meant that the Israelites should no longer offer sacrifices. Nor did Amos mean that when he said that God "hated the feasts" (Amos 5.21).

What both writers meant was this:
  1. Not even sacrifices could restore the relationship between themselves and God which they had spoilt by sin. Nothing that human beings could do would be effective. Only God the merciful judge could do that.
  2. Actions such as making a sacrifice or attending public worship (or having a baby baptized) do not themselves restore the relationship between God and the worshippers. They are not magic. What these actions do is to strengthen this relationship when it already exists.

See also Psalm 40.6–8, in which the writer says that offering oneself in obedience to God ("Lo, I come", v. 7) is far more important than offering sacrifice. The author of Hebrews 10.5–10 quotes Psalm 40 when speaking of Christ as the one Person whose self-offering had been perfect.

*Note:* At an earlier time Psalm 40 had probably been two psalms:
Vv. 1–12:   First psalm—Thanksgiving for deliverance.
Vv. 13–17:   Second psalm—A cry for help.

**Ps. 51.17: A broken spirit.** A Canadian who lived alone liked people to call him "Independence Number One". He had a rule that he would not let anyone else help him to grow his food. When he was taken ill he had to break this rule and allow a neighbour to help him. As a result they became friends. He had not only broken a rule, he had also broken a false idea about himself, namely that he needed no help.

This story shows in some way what a "broken spirit" is, which every man needs before he can received God's forgiveness. It is not that God is jealous of men's strength and likes to see them humiliated and broken down. It is simply that, although this gift of forgiveness is free, people cannot receive it until they are ready to give up the pretence that they are independent.

**Ps. 51.19: Then wilt thou delight in right sacrifices.** Most scholars think that an editor living in the time of Haggai added these two verses (18 and 19) to the psalm. At that time the Israelites had returned from their exile in Babylon and were busily rebuilding the walls of Jerusalem and beginning again to offer sacrifices there. If this is so, then it seems that the editor did not understand the meaning of v. 16, and was afraid that it would discourage people from joining in the sacrifices.

## STUDY SUGGESTIONS

WORDS
1. Make a list of *ten* one-word verbs used in the RSV version of Psalm 51 which express what the writer wanted God to do for him.
2. (a) Give the translation of the following words in
   (i) another English version
   (ii) another language
   steadfast love (v. 1);   mercy (v. 1);   sin (v. 2);   sins (v. 9)
   (b) From your own experience of guilt and of God's forgiving love, which of the translations do you think is the most satisfactory, and why?
3. What is the difference:
   (a) Between sin and shame?
   (b) Between sin and crime?
   (c) Between sin and sins?

CONTENT
4. In which verses of Psalm 51 do we find that the writer:
   (a) Faces the truth about himself, even truth that is painful?
   (b) Expresses his dependence upon God?
   (c) Offers himself to serve God?
5. What is the meaning of:
   (a) "In sin did my mother conceive me" (51.5)?
   (b) "A broken spirit" (51.17)?

6. Give two important truths about God which the writer of Psalm 51 had recognized.

BIBLE

7. "Put a new and right spirit within me" (51.10).
What is the result of God's Spirit meeting with man's spirit in each of the following passages?
(a) Exod. 31.3   (b) 1 Sam. 11.6   (c) Ezek. 37.1–10
(d) Micah 3.8

8. Each of the following passages contains a thought which we also find in Psalm 51. In each case say:
(i) What is that thought?
(ii) In which verse or verses of Psalm 51 do we find it expressed?
(a) Job 15.14   (b) Ps. 38.18   (c) Isa. 65   (d) Ezek. 11.19
(e) Hos. 6.6   (f) Acts 22.16

9. A verse in 2 Samuel 12.1–13 (part of the story of David and Uriah) is very like a verse in Psalm 51. Which are these two verses?

10. Psalms 38 and 51 are alike in several ways. Give two ways in which they are different.

DISCUSSION AND RESEARCH

11. "False guilt, i.e. when we feel guilty although there is no real reason to feel guilty" (p. 60). Give an example from your own experience of someone suffering from this "false" guilt-feeling.

12. "Human beings try all sorts of unsuccessful ways of dealing with the feeling of personal guilt" (p. 60). In your experience, what do people most often do, who cannot believe that they are forgiven?

13. "They believed that such outward symbolic actions had an effect on their relationship with God" (p. 64).
(a) Give one example of an outward symbolic action performed during Temple services.
(b) Give one example of an outward symbolic action which is performed in the services of your own Church today.
(c) In what way, if at all, does this action have an effect on the relationship of yourself and your fellow-worshippers with God?

14. "God is not more masculine than He is feminine" (p. 64).
What is your opinion of the Christian custom of only using masculine words ("He", "Father") when referring to God?

15. "Blot out my transgressions" (Ps. 51.1)
In one Nigerian College the chaplain asked those who were about to be confirmed to write down privately on a piece of paper things in their lives of which they were ashamed. They did this, and then together asked for God's forgiveness. Then each of them burnt

their papers, put the ashes on the altar, and gave thanks for God's renewal.

(a) How helpful do you think these symbolic actions would be?

(b) Suggest, if you can, other ways of achieving the same object.

16. What two reasons does a Christian have for believing that God forgives him, which the writer of Psalm 51 did not have?

# Water in a Dry Land
# Psalm 63

## THEME

### 1. THE EXPERIENCE: LIVING AMONG ENEMIES

All human beings have this experience. Even the most friendly men and women are at times afraid of other people and angry with them. They feel, rightly or wrongly, that these people are harmful.

1. The "enemies" may be individuals whose behaviour seems to be harmful to us. One boy feels this about his parents: he wants to receive training as a musician, but they are preventing him from doing so; they do not take him seriously, and tell him to go and work in an office. A girl who works in a factory feels that her superior is an "enemy" because he discourages her and criticizes her work however well she does it. A young man has a work-mate who gets promotion which the young man had hoped to get, and marries the girl whom the young man had hoped to marry. A newly-appointed headmaster finds that the members of his staff oppose every suggestion which he makes: he feels they are his "enemies".

2. The "enemies" may belong to a group which has been harmful to us, or which (we fear) is still harmful. One man owns a newspaper shop in a small town and the people whom he most fears are a group of men who have just opened a second newspaper shop. They plan to take away the man's trade. The "enemy" group may be another nation or tribe. An engineer in the Philippines who was preparing to go to Japan recently on business wrote: "You ask what I feel about the Japanese. Well, I can only say this, that they killed my father in the war when I was three years old."

During the civil war in Nigeria (1967–70), people living in the West and the North were on the side of the "Federal" Government. A group of those living in the East, mostly belonging to the Ibo tribe, were on the other side, calling themselves "Biafrans". The Federals called the Biafrans "rebels", and accused them of having murdered the Federal and Northern and Western Prime Ministers. The Biafrans called the

Federals "vandals", and accused them of having murdered 30,000 of the Ibo tribe in 1966. People who lived in one part of Nigeria at that time saw the people of the other part as "the enemy", the bad people.

3. The "enemy" may even be people who believe in God but who seem to us to be working against the truth. Many Christians regard those who practise "racialism" as real enemies, e.g. in the USA or South Africa, because such people deny the truth that God made the human family as one family.

4. We have so far thought of "enemies" as being people. But for millions of men and women the chief enemies are invisible evil spirits. They believe that these spirits are working against them through natural objects such as great trees or mountains, or through events such as a thunderstorm or an infectious disease.

A girl in a teacher-training college in Northern Nigeria was ill and, to other people's surprise, did not recover. Then she told a friend that she was the only child in her family who was still alive. She said that the spirits of dead people were all round her, trying to take her away from this world. The friend gave her verse 8 of Psalm 63 to repeat, "My soul clings to *thee*".

Many others, who do not believe in separate evil spirits, nevertheless believe that there is invisible power working to bring disorder into God's ordered world. "Our fight is not against human foes, but against . . . the superhuman forces of evil" (Eph. 6.12, NEB).

In the face of such "enemies" what do people do? The following are a few of the ways in which people behave:

1. They express their hatred and anger. They may do this by word or by action. They may control their feelings or fail to control them.

2. They have angry thoughts about "the enemy", but do not express them outwardly.

3. They push their real feelings and thoughts away and imagine that they do not have such feelings. This often happens, for instance, when people depend on someone else, e.g. a workman depends upon his employer. The workman may be so afraid of losing his job that he does not wish to complain even when the employer treats him unjustly.

4. They submit to the "enemy" in despair.

5. They commit the matter into God's hands and so "forgive" their enemies. See note below on p. 75.

The worshippers in Psalm 63 were praying to God out of some experience of living among enemies, "Those who seek to destroy my life" (v. 9). It seems likely that this psalm was first used by the congregation on behalf of their king, or by the king leading the congregation. We do not know whether the king's enemies were disloyal subjects or national enemies of the Israelites, or worshippers of foreign gods, or people who practised magic.

Whoever the enemy was, the worshippers were able to make this experience part of their worship. They could do this because in that experience they had recognized God as their rescuer.

## 2. THE RECOGNITION OF GOD

As they faced their enemies the worshippers realized three truths about God:

1. God was their own God and they belonged to Him, "O God, *my* God" (v. 1).

2. God loved them more than they deserved. He had shown His "steadfast love" towards them in the past because they were joined to Him by the "Covenant". And He would go on showing it. See note on "steadfast love", Hebrew: *chesed*, on p. 37. This love was so precious to them that they would rather die than live without it. ("It is better than life" (v. 3a).)

3. God was able to protect them against the forces of evil. Note the words "power" (v. 2), "help" (v. 7), and "right hand" (v. 8). For a note on "right hand" see note below on v. 8.

The worshippers explain in the psalm that they are able to hold to this confidence in God because they experience His presence in corporate worship. "I have looked upon thee in the sanctuary" (v. 2), i.e. "I have been present at the Temple worship when we have regularly acknowledged your power and glory".

## 3. THE RESPONSE

Psalm 63 is a response by worshippers who knew that they depended upon God and trusted Him to rescue them. It is in three parts:

**Vv. 1–4:** *Dependence*—Lord, we feel weak and faint because our enemies are so strong. We need you as much as we and our sheep and cattle need water in the dry season.

**Vv. 5–8:** *Confidence*—Lord, we believe you are supporting us. We believe this at all times, both at home ("upon my bed", v. 6), and when we see the carved wings on the Ark of the Covenant in Temple worship ("under the shadow of thy wings", v. 7). See General Note A, p. 48 and note on p. 99.

**Vv. 9–11:** *Confidence* in the face of enemies—Lord, we believe you can prevent our enemies from overwhelming us. "Those who seek to destroy my life shall go down into the depths of the earth" (v. 9). St Paul said, "If God is for us, who is against us?" (Rom. 8.31). See p. 74 for a further comment on these words.

The writer of Psalm 36 made a similar response to God out of an experience of living among enemies.

In vv. 1–4 he simply refers to "the enemy".

In vv. 5–9 he expresses confidence in God. (This part by itself provides

"It is good to hate evil and to fight against it" (p. 74).

Political demonstrators in Chile were protesting against social oppression, and demanding "land, freedom, and justice".

In what ways, if any, should the methods of Christians who are fighting injustice be different from methods used by political parties?

a good short hymn of praise, e.g. "with thee is the fountain of life; in thy light do we see light", v. 9.)

In vv. 10–12 he repeats his confidence in God in spite of the enemies.

## USE

1. We have already seen that the Israelite king himself may have used this psalm. Most people think, from the following phrases, that it was used in the Temple:

**V. 2a.** I have looked upon thee in the sanctuary.

**V. 2b.** Beholding thy power and glory. See note on Psalm 8.1b, 2.

**V. 4a.** I will lift up my hands. The Israelite worshippers often prayed standing up, with the palms of their hands facing upwards.

**V. 4b.** Call on thy name. See note on Psalm 8.1b.

**V. 7.** In the shadow of thy wings. See General Note A, p. 48.

Some people believe that as part of the worship there was a symbolic fight. This was a way of showing that God would overcome evil.

2. It is possible for a Christian congregation to use the whole of Psalm 63 if members interpret vv. 9–11 in some such way as the following: "the power of God will overcome the evil in the world and n ourselves".

But it is easy to use these verses in the wrong way. If someone feels that one of his fellow-workers is an "enemy" or if a small group of Christians is being persecuted by non-Christians, they would be tempted to use these verses as a prayer of hate. See note on Psalm 139.19. In this case it would be better to use vv. 1–8 only, even though, by doing so, they would be missing the main meaning of the psalm.

3. Psalm 63 has been very often used in private. The first six words, "O God, thou art my God", make a good arrow prayer with which to start the day and perhaps no more words are needed. (If we follow the Hebrew closely, we should translate this, "O God, my God, Thee, Thee do I seek".) A girl nursing a friend who was suffering from serious mental illness found this work very hard. She could only sleep for a few hours each night. "My prayer-time", she said, "was spent simply drinking deep of God and saying 'God, you are my God'." St Chrysostom, the great theologian, used these words more than the words of any other psalm.

## NOTES

**Ps. 63.5: My soul is feasted.** Loving and obeying God satisfies the one who loves Him. Jesus said, "It is meat and drink for me to do the will of him who sent me" (John 4.34).

It may often seem that loving God is only giving service to Him in worship, or in service to our fellow human beings for His sake. But it is God's plan that the person who loves also receives satisfaction, so that he can say: "I was made for this! In giving myself to God in this way I become my fullest self."

In this verse the writer says that to love God is as satisfying as it is to eat fat. Often there was not much fat on the Israelites' animals, and as a result fat was particularly valuable to them.

**Ps. 63.8: Thy right hand upholds me.** In the Bible, writers use the words "right hand" in the following ways:

(a) Most people are right-handed, so that people show their strength with the tools or weapons used in their right hands. An accident to either hand is serious, but an accident to the right hand extremely serious. The king's "right hand" in Psalm 45.4 means his power to defeat enemies.

(b) The phrase is used to mean the power by which God creates and sustains the world. "My right hand spread out the heavens" (Isa. 48.13).

(c) Most often it means the power by which God rescues His people. "O saviour of those who seek refuge at thy right hand" (Ps. 17.7).

(d) In many countries people use the right hand as a sign of giving honour to others. Similarly in the Bible, to be "at God's right hand" means to share God's honour and authority. When St Peter wanted to say that God had made Jesus "Lord", he quoted Psalm 110.1, "The Lord said to my Lord, sit at my right hand".

**Ps. 63.9: Those who seek to destroy my life shall go down.** There are several psalms like Psalm 63, in which the writer asks God to punish his enemies, "Let ruin come upon them" (Ps. 35.8), "Consume them in wrath (Ps. 59.13). "Let them be blotted out" (Ps. 69.28), "May his children wander about and beg" (Ps. 109.10), "Let burning coals fall upon them" (Ps. 140.10).

What are we to say about prayers of this kind?

1. *It is good to hate evil and to fight against it.* The Christian Dr Martin Luther King fought against those who prevented negroes in the USA from obtaining good homes and education and work. Because of his fight he was shot dead in 1968. If we fail to hate evil, we are unlikely to fight it. If we do not fight it, how will the evil be overcome?

Those who first used Psalm 63 believed that they fought against national enemies, rather than against "evil" in general. But they thought of themselves as God's "chosen people", and thought of the king as God's representative. Therefore when they fought against their national enemies, they believed they were on the side of right and against the side of wrong. This verse 9 is thus a prayer that God would judge between right and wrong. (Of course the Israelite king who was fighting a national enemy was not always on the side of right. According to Amos it was sometimes the national enemies of the Israelites who were on God's side (Amos 6.8; 9.4).)

74

2. *Evil is not a person, but the disease called sin.* When people brought to Jesus a woman whom they knew to be a "sinner", Jesus had compassion on the woman herself but hated her sinfulness (John 8.3–11). A story from Eastern Europe may help to illustrate this. An officer of the police was cruelly questioning a political prisoner, a woman, throughout the whole of one night. Clearly this officer was the woman's enemy. But during the questioning she realized that the officer was working under an evil system from which he could not get free. When she saw this, she felt that her real enemy was not the officer, but the sinfulness of the way in which the whole country was governed.

3. *Evil is in ourselves as in other people.* The writer of Psalm 51 understood this: "Have mercy on *me*" (v. 1). For him, and for Christians, the fight was as much against evil in himself as against evil which was at work in other people. This does not mean that we should accuse ourselves of being worse than others. It means that we should know clearly what we are. See Matthew 7.5.

But the writers of some other psalms (perhaps the writer of Psalm 63 was one of these) did not understand this. They felt, "God, we are on your side and therefore we are good. They (the enemy) are on the other side and are therefore bad". They were like the Pharisee of whom Jesus spoke (Luke 18.10–14) who said, "God, I thank thee that I am not like other men."

4. *Jesus gave His followers new teaching* which was not in the mind of the writer of Psalm 63. He taught them to forgive their enemies. This teaching was based on the following truths:

(a) God has forgiven us who do not deserve to be forgiven. "While we were yet sinners, Christ died for us" (Rom. 5.8).

(b) If it is right for us to receive God's forgiveness, then it is right for us to forgive other people, even when we feel that they do not deserve it. "Forgiving one another as God in Christ forgave you" (Eph. 4.32).

(c) When God forgives us, it is because He wants our well-being rather than our downfall. When we forgive other people we are wanting their well-being. We are also doing two other things:

We are giving up the pleasure of feeling superior to them (superior because we are right and they are wrong).

We are putting the case into God's hands. If they must be punished, it is for God, not us, to punish them. "I (not you) will repay, saith the Lord" (Rom. 12.19).

(d) When we forgive our enemies, they do not always cease to be enemies. It may be right and necessary to oppose them. The father of a family in Uganda had a neighbour who drove his motor-cycle dangerously and once injured the father's young son. The father managed to forgive the neighbour, but whenever he saw him driving too fast he protested very strongly.

5. There are times when we have been so badly hurt that we feel we cannot forgive the person who did the injury. What are we to do? We are to share this with God: "Lord God, I am not forgiving this person. But I believe that You have forgiven him. Forgive me for not forgiving. Help me to forgive." In this way we shall be following the writer of Psalm 63 who shared with God His pain of living among enemies.

6. *Jesus lived among enemies.* Some of His enemies were: the Jewish religious leaders (John 7.32), a Jewish political leader (Luke 13.32), those who did harm to defenceless people (Mark 9.42), invisible powers (Matthew 10.1), His own friends and disciples (John 6.15). Jesus behaved towards these and His many other enemies in various ways: He opposed them by what He said (John 6.41) and by what He did (Matthew 21.12, 13). He withdrew from them or remained silent (John 6.15, 7.1–9). He submitted to them (John 18.12). He asked God to forgive them (Luke 23.33, 34).

## STUDY SUGGESTIONS

### WORDS

1. In Psalm 63 the writer shows that he is directing his attention to God by addressing Him as "thee" ten times, e.g. in v. 1 he says, "I *seek* thee". What other words besides "seek" does the writer use in order to express the different ways in which he approaches God and addresses his response to Him?

### CONTENT

2. (a) What kind of experience had the writer of Psalm 63 probably had, which led him to write this psalm?
   (b) Why does he say that he is like a thirsty man?
3. Describe *three* different ways in which people behave towards their enemies.
4. What was so precious to the writer of Psalm 63 that he would rather die than lose it?
5. What made it possible for the writer of Psalm 63 to believe that God was loving enough and strong enough to protect him?
6. What is the chief reason why Christians should forgive those who have hurt or harmed them?
7. What can a Christian do who finds that he cannot forgive someone who has hurt or harmed him?

### BIBLE

8. In what two ways is Psalm 63 like the two Psalms 42 and 43?

9. Read again the note on Psalm 63.8. What do the words "right hand" refer to in each of the following verses:
   (a) Ps. 18.35  (b) Ps. 63.8  (c) Ps. 89.13
   (d) Matt. 26.64  (e) Luke 6.6.  (f) Rom. 8.34
10. "Jesus lived among enemies" (p. 76). Who were the enemies of Jesus mentioned in the following passages:
    (a) Mark 3.6  (b) Mark 3.21  (c) Mark 3.22  (d) Mark 14.10
    (e) Mark 14.65  (f) Mark 15.15  (g) Luke 9.52, 53
    (h) Luke 23.11
11. Read the following passages and describe briefly in each case how Jesus behaved towards His enemies:
    (a) Mark 3.5  (b) Mark 7.5  (c) Mark 11.15  (d) Mark 12.15
    (e) Mark 14.43–49  (f) Mark 15.4, 5  (g) Luke 4.28, 29
    (h) Luke 15.2  (i) Luke 23.33, 34  (j) John 8.48–55
12. Psalm 36.5-9 provides "a good short hymn of praise" (p. 73).
    (a) In what way is it "good", in your opinion?
    (b) Suggest one way in which Psalm 36.5-9 could be used in public worship.
    (c) Which verses of Psalm 63 are like Psalm 36.5-9?

DISCUSSION AND RESEARCH

13. "Loving God satisfies the one who loves Him" (p. 73).
    (a) On which verse of Psalm 63 was this comment based?
    (b) Under what conditions, in your experience, is daily work "satisfying"?
    (c) Under what conditions does public worship become "satisfying"?
    (d) What is the difference between being satisfied and content on the one hand, and being self-satisfied on the other hand?
14. Give one example, if you can, from everyday life, of each of the following:
    (a) A personal enemy.  (b) People who are enemies because they belong to a group which seems harmful or dangerous.  (c) People who are "enemies" because they seem to be working against God's truth.
15. "When we forgive our enemies, they do not always cease to be enemies. It may be right and necessary to oppose them" (p. 75).
    (a) What is your opinion?
    (b) Give an example from everyday life to illustrate your answer.
16. "Dr Martin Luther King fought . . ." (p. 74). Give examples of as many individuals as you can, who in different parts of the world are fighting in the name of Jesus Christ against those who seem to be treating their fellow human-beings unjustly.
17. (a) If you were leading public worship, could you use all of Psalm

63, *or* part of it, *or* none of it? Give reasons for your answer.
(b) If you used Psalm 63 at all, *how* would you use it? (e.g. would
you sing or say it? Would everybody join in?)
18. A college teacher said of a student, "He is his own worst enemy."
(a) What do you think the teacher meant?
(b) How far is it true to say this about anyone?

# The Harvest
# Psalm 67

## THEME

### 1. THE EXPERIENCE: PROSPERITY

Some members of a Christian congregation in Indonesia were accustomed to meet and talk together after the Church service. One Sunday
they were all feeling gloomy because a storm had damaged their church
roof. Then someone said, "Instead of complaining about this misfor-
tune, let us tell each other about the things that have given us pleasure
since we last met." These are the "things" they spoke about:

One man who was a clerk said he had just had a rise in salary.
Another said that for the first time for a year all his family had been
home at the same time. A third had been able to buy a bigger house.
A fourth had had a letter from a son abroad. A fifth had bought a new
suit. One woman who had been shopping had got a place on the crowded
bus; another spoke of "hot water to wash in when I didn't expect it".
A gardener referred to the rain throughout the district, and his friend
had had a large crop of vegetables. A student had passed his examination. A girl had earned her first wages.

These people had all experienced the enjoyment of very ordinary
things; they had experienced "prosperity".

There are many possible ways in which we behave when we experience
"prosperity":

(a) One way is to say, "See what I have achieved", i.e. we pretend
that we obtained the good things without the help of anyone else.
"Beware, lest you say in your heart, 'My power and the might of my
hand have gotten me this wealth' " (Deut. 8.17).

(b) Another way is to say, "This is mine, not yours", i.e. we may
compare ourselves with those who possess less than we ourselves possess.
We may even imagine that we are better people because we possess
more things.

(c) A third way to behave is to say, "This above everything else is important in life", i.e. we imagine that having one particular thing is what makes life better. Jesus did not tell people that they ought not to think in this way. He simply explained that it prevented them from having even more valuable gifts from God. "How hard it will be for those who have riches to enter the kingdom of God" (Mark 10.23). A few years ago, a visitor to Sweden said: "The people of Sweden eat better food and live in more comfortable houses than the people of any other country. But I hear that in Sweden more people commit suicide than they do anywhere else, and more married people obtain divorces." It seems as if they have made the mistake of depending too much on material things.

(d) A fourth way is to discover with disappointment that possessions do not themselves make us happy and, as a result, to become "bored" with living. Many of the people who habitually take drugs, such as alcohol or other substances, began the habit because they were "bored" in this way.

(e) A fifth way is the way of those Israelites who worshipped in the words of this psalm. They started from the enjoyment of things (like the members of that Indonesian congregation), and were able to look beyond the things to God the giver.

## 2. THE RECOGNITION OF GOD

(a) They recognized God as *creating and giving* the good things which they experienced. "You shall remember the Lord your God, for it is he who gives you power to get wealth" (Deut. 8.18). See note on Psalm 67.3 on the words "Praise thee".

(b) They also recognized God as their *rescuer*, through His many special deeds which their ancestors had recorded. They recognized Him as the one who not only gave gifts, but who rescued them because He had entered into a personal relationship with them. We discover this from the words and phrases used in the psalm:

(i) "May God be gracious to us . . .". This quotation in v. 1 from Numbers 6.24–6 was the blessing which "Aaron and his sons" proclaimed in God's name. They would not have proclaimed this blessing if an event had not occurred on an earlier occasion, i.e. if Moses had not experienced God on Mount Sinai (Exod. 19.16–25 and Exod. 24). On the mountain God gave Moses the commandments which the Israelites should obey: He made a "Covenant" with Moses, who accepted it on behalf of his people. From that time the Israelites believed that God, who had rescued them from slavery in Egypt, had a "Covenant" with them. See note on Psalm 103.18 The worshippers quoted this "blessing", therefore, because they remembered God's special deeds of rescue.

(ii) They also connected the following important words with special events in their history, events by which they knew of God's plan to save them:

"Gracious" v. 1 ("He has treated us with mercy throughout our history");

"Face" v. 1 ("We know His presence with us as we worship: He is not removed from us");

"Saving power" v. 2 ("He has shown over the years that He has the will and the power to rescue us");

"Judge" v. 4 ("Under His rule we have obtained justice").

From these words we see that those who began by seeing God as the provider of prosperity, also saw that He was much more than that. They saw Him even more clearly as their rescuer or "saviour" in all life, and as One with whom they had a special relationship. See note on Psalm 22.21.

(c) They recognized God as One who was *concerned that other peoples*, as well as themselves, *should enjoy His gifts*. See, for example, "Thy saving power among all nations" (v. 2).

If this psalm contained only one such phrase we might think that it was a poetical way of saying "let God be praised by many people", i.e. by many Israelites. But the idea is repeated six times, probably in order to emphasize the truth that God is concerned with all human beings.

## 3. THE RESPONSE

The response which the worshippers were expressing in this psalm was of several kinds:

(a) *Thanks*. It was a response of thanks to God, as we see in the chorus and in v. 4. "Rejoice and shout in triumph" (NEB). The worshippers did not say this because they believed that God would stop looking after them unless they flattered Him. They simply wished to state the truth: What we have, He gave. "What have you that you did not receive?" (1 Cor. 4.7). Therefore we thank Him. See notes on p. 149 and on Psalm 116.17.

(b) *Dependence*. The worshippers were saying that they continually depended upon God. "May God be gracious" (v. 1), i.e. as we have depended on Him in the past to provide for us and to rescue us, so we continue to do so. "In Him we live and move and have our being" (Acts 17.28).

We may note two other psalms in which worshippers show their dependence on God, either just before or after Harvest time.

Psalm 65 is in three parts.

Vv. 1–4: Praise to God from worshippers in the Temple courts.

Vv. 5–8: Praise to God, the controller of all creation.

Vv. 9–13: Confidence that God will repeatedly make the soil fertile.

Note also that in Psalm 65 (as in Psalm 67) the writer is concerned for other nations. See v. 5.

Psalm 85 has a similar plan:

Vv. 1–3: Remembrance of what God has done.

Vv. 4–7: Appeal for God's continued support.

Vv. 8–13: Hope in God that He will continue to look after His people.

    (a) *Hope.* They expressed the hope that there would be a time when all God's people would acknowledge Him as Lord. "Let all the ends of the earth fear him" (v. 7). See note on Psalm 98.9.

    (b) *Awe.* They responded to God with awe and respect. This is the meaning of the word "fear" in v. 7. See note on Psalm 67.7.

    The plan of Psalm 67 is as follows:

Vv. 1, 2: Man's dependence on God.

V. 3: Chorus—Praise to God.

V. 4: God's concern for other nations.

V. 5: Chorus.

Vv. 6, 7: Thanksgiving for harvest.

The chorus was probably repeated at the end.


## USE

It seems likely that the Israelites used this psalm as a harvest festival thanksgiving offered by the whole congregation at some time in the autumn (God is called "*our* God" in v. 6). Probably one singer or a choir sang the strophes, and the people shouted or sang the chorus. This is still a good way to sing it, since the chorus is simple and contains the main thought of the Psalm.

Because this Psalm contains reference to people other than Israelites ("*all* the peoples"), some Churches use it at services where there is special prayer for people other than Christians, e.g. at Epiphany, because at this festival Christians remember how people other than Jews brought gifts to Jesus.

The Christian writer *H. F. Lyte* wrote a hymn in about 1820 which is based on this Psalm, but is not a translation. The first verse is as follows:

> God of mercy, God of grace,
> Show the brightness of thy face,
> Shine upon us, Saviour, shine,
> Fill thy Church with light divine;
> And thy saving health extend
> Unto earth's remotest end.


## NOTES

**Ps. 67.1: Bless us.** An Israelite worshipper who said this would probably have some such thoughts as these about God "blessing":

"Thy saving power" (Ps. 67.2).

The pilot of this helicopter from Hong Kong rescued forty-three members of the crew of a ship which had run aground. What do we mean when we call God our "rescuer" or "saviour"?

1. God has both the desire and the power to give us what is good for us.
2. He wishes us to enjoy food, and intends cattle to have calves and parents to have children. In Deuteronomy the phrase God's "blessing" is used especially for gifts such as these (see Deut. 28.1–6). Human beings may deprive themselves of such things, e.g. by fighting each other or by breaking the rules of good farming. But God for His part provides them.
3. God offers His chosen people even more "gifts" than material things like food or wealth, and offers them to those who belong to the worshipping congregation. "Blessed be he who enters . . ." (Ps. 118.26).

*Note:* When people respond to God's blessings by praising Him, they often use the same word "bless", to show that their praise is a response to God's care for them. It is part of the same conversation, so to speak, and so the same word is used. "Bless the Lord, O my soul" (Ps. 103.1). But this can be confusing. God blesses us in ways in which we cannot possibly bless Him. So it is usually better to use the word "praise" for the activity of human beings.

**Ps. 67.2: Thy saving power.** The Hebrew word used here is one of a group of words (*yeshua, yasha,* etc) which Israelites used to refer to God as rescuer or saviour. See note on Psalm 22.21. The name which we pronounce Jesus or Yesu comes from these words.

*From what* does God save us, according to the writers in the Bible? Both from "material" evils, such as enemies and illness and famine and prison, and from "spiritual" evil, i.e. from the state of being a stranger in the presence of God because of our sin. It is chiefly in the New Testament that we read of the second of these.

*What* is salvation? It is God setting people free, restoring them, giving them completeness in their lives. Compare the note on "peace" (Ps. 72.7).

*Whom* does God save? Many Old Testament writers refer to their whole nation being saved (Ps. 118.25), and God is indeed concerned to give salvation (i.e. peace and completeness) to the groups in which people live, whether nations or families or Church congregations. Others, and especially New Testament writers, are concerned about the salvation of individuals.

*Through whom* does God save? Although it is always God who saves, there were Israelite leaders whom God used, e.g. Moses in Egypt. The New Testament is of course the story of how God saves in a unique way "through Jesus Christ" (Acts 4.12).

*Is salvation complete?* In some ways it is complete. God saved the Israelites from Egypt and they did not go back. And Paul said in Ephesians 2.8: "You have been saved." But the completion of God's saving also lies in the future. See 1 Corinthians 1.18, "those who are being saved." See note on Psalm 98.9.

**Ps. 67.2: Among all nations.** Not many writers of Psalms express this concern for other peoples, which we have already noticed on p. 81. One reason is the special relationship and Covenant which the Israelites had with God. They were afraid that if they mixed with other tribes, they could not remain faithful to Him. When, later on, God showed them that they were responsible for caring for other tribes, they were often unwilling to do so. An unknown teacher recorded the story of Jonah especially to remind them of this responsibility. "Arise and go to Nineveh . . . and proclaim to it the message that I tell you" (Jonah 3.2). See notes on Psalms 96.3 and 100.1.

Christians have special reason to share what they value with other people, i.e. with other Christians and with members of other religions.

At harvest time Christians show that they are grateful to God by dedicating themselves to share what they possess, and to work for the fair sharing of the world's food "among all nations". When the members of a Christian congregation distribute harvest offerings among the poor people of their neighbourhood, such distribution is a sign that they are grateful to God.

A visitor to Kenya recently watched the end of a Harvest Festival service. "They came rushing out, carrying cabbages, maize, beans, sweet potatoes, and went singing down the road. Two children carried eggs and blankets to the hut of a very old man and woman. A girl named Mercy gave the woman a blanket and told her why we had come. Then the boy put an egg gently in her husband's hands, and the old man held it as if it was gold."

But God calls on Christians to share everything they most value, not only a good harvest. And this naturally includes what they believe about God and His Son Jesus. So every Christian has to work out how to share his belief with other people.

A Christian college-lecturer working in a Muslim part of India goes once a week to the mosque where the maulvi (or "minister") lives. He sits on a string bed and listens and talks and asks questions for an hour or two. Each shares with the other what he believes.

When we share what we value we are sometimes accused of "interfering" in other people's lives. The students who are taught by the lecturer referred to above told him, "When we went into the villages last month people thought at first that we had come to preach, and they were hostile. Then they saw that we had come to make friends."

**Ps. 67.2, 6: Thy saving power . . . the earth has yielded.** These two phrases stand for two rather different acts of worship. The first phrase expresses our recognition of God who has saved His people in special ways at special times; the second expresses our belief that God continually acts towards us with generosity.

(a) Some Christians call the first "the worship of the God of grace", e.g. of God who, in His special generosity, came into a special part of the world (Palestine) in a way that has not been repeated. We remember this particularly at Christmas. In such worship we think of God mainly as Saviour.

(b) We may call the second sort the "worship of the God of nature", i.e. of God who causes natural events such as harvest, to be repeated year after year. Many Churches have services for such events as New Year's Day, the Sowing of Crops, the Gathering of the First Fruits. At such times we think of God as Creator.

The truth about God is that He both "saves" and "creates". Those who plan the services of the Church must show both sides of this truth.

**Ps. 67.3: Praise thee.** The Israelites recognized that there is a power (God) who is beyond human beings, who (or which) provides the harvest. So they sang "praise *thee*".

In believing this they were like people throughout the world who follow the traditional religion of their tribe or nation, not one of the major world religions such as Judaism, Islam, Hinduism, Buddhism, Christianity. Most of such people believe in a High God, and perform special ritual actions because they believe that in this way their wives, their cattle, and their fields will receive fertility from this High God. The Canaanites, the occupiers of the land which the Israelites invaded, held this kind of belief about their god, and called him "Baal". But the Israelites, as we have seen, were able to see more about God than the Baal-worshippers did. And Christians have still more reason to praise God for harvest. But today some people feel that it is more difficult than it used to be to praise and thank God wholeheartedly for the things they enjoy. Many people in the cities today do not grow their own rice. They go into shops and buy rice which has been cleaned by machinery and packed (perhaps also by a machine) in a paper bag. These people sometimes feel that it is human beings with their machines rather than God who have provided the rice. When everyone saw the rice growing in the paddy fields it was easier for them to think of God as the provider.

Another reason why some people find it difficult to recognize God as the giver of good things is this: they have been taught that God does not regard material things like food and clothes as important. They think that God only regards the welfare of mind and spirit as important. But we do not find such teaching in either the Old or New Testament. Jesus thought that giving someone a cup of *water* was very important (Matt. 10.42). And He taught us to pray "Give us this day our daily *bread*" (Matt. 6.11).

**Ps. 67.7: Fear him.** See note on Psalm 130.4b, p. 162. There was a time when Israelites, like the pagans around them, had felt terror in the presence of God as in the presence of a mysterious or an unfriendly power. But because of the way in which He had treated them, they came to see that God had a special and personal relationship with them. So they reverenced Him instead of being terrified.

Christians feel a deep reverence and respect for God's supreme authority. A woman who earned her living as a cook described this respect for God very clearly: she said that her respect for Him was like her respect for the fire. But God has shown more of Himself to us than that. When people saw Jesus they were seeing God. And Jesus was a person, and a person who loved and cared for the people around Him. So we see not only God's authority, we see His love. And His perfect love casts out our terror. See 1 John 4.18.

## STUDY SUGGESTIONS

### WORDS

1. (a) What is the difference in meaning between the following two groups of words:
   (i) dread   dismay   terror   anxiety
   (ii) worship   wonder   awe   reverence   respect
   (b) Which group best describes the attitude to God of the Israelite worshippers who used Psalm 67?
   (c) Say which words in the psalm you have noticed in giving your answer to (b).

### CONTENT

2. Those who used this psalm recognized the activity of God as they enjoyed their harvest. What *three* things about God did they recognize?
3. What is the most important way in which a Harvest Festival is a different act of worship from a Christmas Day service?
4. "The Israelites were able to see more about God than the Baal-worshippers did" (p. 85). What "more" did they see?
5. "Thy saving power" (Ps. 67.2)
   From what does God save us, according to the writers in the Bible?

### BIBLE STUDY

6. In each of the following pairs of passages from the Psalms there is one truth which we have noticed in Psalm 67. Say in each case what that truth is:
   (a) Ps. 22.27, 28 and Ps. 47.5–9
   (b) Ps. 65.9–13 and Ps. 85.10–13
7. The Israelites connected important words such as "gracious", "face", "saving power", and "judge" with special events in their

history, "events by which they knew of God's plan to save them" (p. 80).

(i) Of what events do we read in the following passages:

(a) 2 Kings 13.22, 23

(b) 2 Chron. 32.9–11 and 20–23

(c) Ps. 105.1–4 and 26–38

(d) Ps. 106.1–9

(ii) In which verses of those passages do we find any of these "important words" or others with similar meaning?

8. "God offers His chosen people even better gifts than material things" (p. 83).

Many of these "better gifts" or "blessings" are mentioned in Psalm 118. Give 3 examples of them.

## DISCUSSION AND RESEARCH

9. Give examples from everyday life of *two* of the ways in which people behave in times of prosperity, as described on pp. 78, 79.

10. "Every Christian has to work out how to share his belief with other people". How can we do so without interfering with other people's lives or suggesting that their beliefs are foolish?

11. "When everyone saw the rice growing in the paddy fields, it was easier for them to think of God as the provider" (p. 85), i.e. it was easier than when we buy it in a bag from a shopkeeper.

(a) What is your opinion?

(b) If the statement is true, what can a Christian do in order to recognize God as the giver of good things?

12. During a Harvest sermon a preacher said, "It is more Christian to praise God for His own sake and for His own nature than to thank Him for material prosperity." What is your opinion?

13. A woman said that her "respect for God was like her respect for the fire" (p. 86).

(a) What is your opinion of that illustration?

(b) Give two other illustrations from everyday life to show the meaning of "respect for God".

14. Choose one popular Harvest hymn which your Church uses, and read it through carefully.

(a) What truths are missing from that hymn which we find in Psalm 67?

(b) What truths are expressed in that hymn which are missing from Psalm 67?

15. What reply would you make to someone who said, "If I thanked God for a good harvest, I should be saying that God had made me a favourite and that I deserved success more than the people who had a bad harvest. I cannot thank God for harvest."

16. The note on Psalm 67.2 (p. 83) refers to God's being "concerned to give salvation (i.e. peace and completeness) to the *groups* in which people live", and it refers also to "God's salvation of *individuals*".
(a) To which of these two was the writer of Psalm 67 referring?
(b) Which of them do you think to be the more important? Give your reasons.

# The King
# Psalm 72

## THEME

### 1. THE EXPERIENCE: BELONGING

It is difficult to imagine what it would be like to live entirely without other people and to belong to no group of fellow human-beings. Our minds would be damaged, just as our bodies are damaged if we go for too long without food.

Everyone who reads this has, since childhood, had the experience of "belonging". At first he probably felt that he belonged to "mother". Later he knew that he belonged to his whole family, to mother and father and brothers and sisters and the rest. Later there were other groups, a class in school, a games team, an "age-group", a Church congregation. At some point he discovered that he belonged also to another group, one which he had never seen as a group because it was so large and so widely scattered, namely the people of his country, his "nation".

Our experiences of belonging sometimes bring us joy, sometimes pain. The group (or its leader) may enable us to grow and develop in character, or it may overwhelm us and prevent our growth. Again the group may make too many demands on us, or too few demands. But belonging is one of the very important experiences in life.

Those who first worshipped God with the words of Psalm 72 worshipped Him out of the experience of belonging.

1. They belonged, above all, to the People of Israel, whose visible leader was the king. To belong to this "People" mattered more to the Israelites than anything else. The most terrible thing that could happen to an Israelite was to be excluded from membership. Israelites were excluded if, for instance, they had touched a dead body, unless they received cleansing according to the law (Num. 19.11–20).

2. The People of Israel to which they belonged was both a "state"

or "nation" and a "Church". Two things followed from this: (a) To be a member of the nation was to be a member of the religious body. A national assembly was also a religious assembly. (b) The political head was also the religious head. Nevertheless, there were certain times when the Israelites were aware of belonging to the nation in *all* its activities, as they were when they used Psalm 72. And there were other times when they were chiefly aware of belonging to the nation at its Temple worship, as they were when they used Psalm 100. For this reason we study Psalm 100 separately in this book, although it, like Psalm 72, arose out of the experience of "belonging".

3. For the Israelites it was so important to belong to the nation and to the king that they were tempted to think that nothing in the world, not even the will of God, was important except their nation. This is the reason why Samuel refused to give the Israelites a king when they first asked him (see 1 Sam. 10.17–19). When he did allow them to have a king, he warned them that things would only go well for the nation "if both you and the king who reigns over you will follow the Lord your God" (1 Sam. 12.14, 15). We are reminded of the West African story and proverb which says that there is "No king as God".

To "follow the Lord" is just what the writer of Psalm 72 was leading the worshippers to do.

## 2. THE RECOGNITION OF GOD

Although the name of God only occurs twice in Psalm 72, the whole psalm is a recognition of God as Supreme King. The worshippers acknowledge that:

1. It is God who makes a leader a good leader. "Justice" and "righteousness" which a good leader shows are qualities which God Himself shows towards the Israelites, "Give the king *thy* justice, O God" (v. 1).

"Justice" means a knowledge of what is right and the power to see that right is done. See note on p. 107. "Righteousness" means creating peace by means of a loving concern for people.

2. God is the King of all kings. Therefore the leader of the nation is subject to God. Because of the Covenant he is anwerable to God for the way he uses his authority. "Blessed be the God of Israel who *alone* does wondrous things" (v. 18).

## 3. THE RESPONSE

Since God was king over both ruler and people, the worshippers in Psalm 72 acknowledge God as Supreme King and pray to Him for their national ruler. This prayer for the king (vv. 3–17) is also a message for the people, or "prophecy", because it proclaims the truth as the Hebrew prophets proclaimed it, i.e.: "According to the covenant

"Belonging is one of the very important experiences in life" (p. 88).

These African villagers have banded themselves together to build a dam across the river with their own hands. As a result, the whole community will have water all the year round.

between God and ourselves, we know that there will be peace in our land if we are loyal to God".

The Psalm is in six short parts:

**Vv. 1, 2:** Praise to God the King of kings.

**Vv. 3–7:** Prayer that the ruler may be "righteous", that the land may be fertile, and that there may be justice for all sections of the community.

**Vv. 8–11:** Prayer that the king may be strong, and that since he is God's representative, his power may extend over other nations.

**Vv. 12–15:** Further prayer that the king may be righteous.

**Vv. 16, 17:** Further prayer that the land may be fertile.

**Vv. 18, 19:** Further praise to God.

When the psalms were divided into five books, this psalm was the last psalm of Book 2. Many people believe that the editor of that time added vv. 18 and 19 as his own conclusion to the whole of Book 2. This may be so. But these verses do in fact sum up clearly the theme of Psalm 72 itself.

## USE

1. At first Psalm 72 seems to have been a "Royal Psalm", i.e. a prayer for an Israelite king. Probably it was used at his enthronement. (The enthronement of Solomon is described in 1 Kings 1.33–40, when "all the people went up after him playing on pipes, and rejoicing with great joy, so that the earth was split by their noise".) See note on Royal Psalms on p. 47. Afterwards it was probably used regularly as a prayer for the king and the nation.

Another Royal Psalm is Psalm 2. Its plan is:

**Vv. 1–3:** God and the Israelite king have their enemies.

**Vv. 4–6:** God will subdue opposition to his will.

**Vv. 7–12:** "God has appointed me to be His 'son' and to overcome evil." This part was spoken by the king. Christians who use Psalm 72 usually do so believing that Jesus Christ has in fact come as the King who is fully God's "Son".

2. Perhaps Psalm 72 was also part of the Israelites' annual festival of the Enthronement of God as King. See General Note A, p. 46 and note on p. 109.

3. But later verses like v. 17 "May his name endure for ever" were emphasized, and people said, "These words do not fit a human king, not even a king who was made God's special servant when he was anointed. They point to a 'Messiah' whom God will send to save us from evil."

Since the coming of Jesus Christ, Christians have used this psalm in two different ways:

(a) They have used it as an act of praise to Jesus. It is natural to do this since Jesus is the Messiah for whom some of the Israelites were waiting.

Two hymns which are much used today are based on this psalm and on the interpretation that Jesus is King. The first verse of one of these hymns is based on vv. 2 and 4 of this psalm:

> Hail to the Lord's Anointed,
> Great David's greater Son!
> Hail, in the time appointed,
> His reign on earth begun!
> He comes to break oppression,
> To set the captive free,
> To take away transgression,
> And rule in equity.

The first verse of the other hymn is based on vv. 5 and 8:

> Jesus shall reign where'er the sun
> Doth his successive journeys run;
> His Kingdom stretch from shore to shore,
> Till suns shall rise and set no more.

(b) Christians have used Psalm 72 as a prayer for the nation and for those in authority in the land. In one church they used the psalm in the following way. The first reader quoted a certain verse from the psalm, the second reader interpreted it. After each pair of readings, the minister said the versicle, and the people made the response. For example:

*1st Reader:* Give the king thy justice O God (v. 1).
*2nd Reader:* May our rulers know that their authority is thy gift and that they must give to Thee account of their rule.
*Versicle:* Blessed be the Lord (v. 18a).
*Response:* May his glory fill the whole earth (v. 19b).


## NOTES

**Ps. 72.1a: Give the king thy justice.** The Israelites thanked God for "order" more than for any other of His gifts, as we saw in the study of Psalm 19. The thing they were most afraid of was "chaos", a return to the state of being "without form" (Gen. 1.2). For this reason God has let each group of human beings have a leader. In this verse we see that it is God who gives the authority to whatever human being is leader. For his part the leader is responsible to God for the way he uses this authority.

This is true of the head of a government. It is what St Paul had in mind when he wrote, "Let every person be subject to the governing authorities. For there is no authority except from God..." (Rom 13.1). It is true of the head of a family, the captain of a games team, the headmaster of a school, the minister of a congregation. Each is free to exercise his authority in the way that seems best. He may act in consultation with members of his group, but the authority is his, and he may not give it away so long as he holds the position of leader. For example, parents are the leaders of the family group. If they are free to choose they must not give their authority away to anyone else, e.g. in the matter of the religious education of their children, neither to the school nor the state nor the Church. These organizations exist to help parents to exercise their authority, not to take authority away from the parents.

What has been written above applies to the period during which someone holds his position as leader. Some readers may ask questions which we have not tried to answer here, e.g. by what means and for what reasons should the members of a group replace the leader?

**Ps. 72.1b: Give thy righteousness to the royal son.** This "royal son" is the king of whom we read in the first part of this verse, not that king's son. This becomes clear when we remember that throughout the psalms writers use "parallel" sentences and "parallel" verses, i.e. the writer repeats in the second of two lines or verses what he has said in the first, but using different words. See note 2 on Psalm 8.4. In this verse line 2 is "parallel" to line 1. We see this kind of "parallelism" in all of the short verses of this psalm.

**Ps. 72.3: Let the mountains bear prosperity . . . in righteousness.** Some readers may be surprised to read that if the ruler is "righteous" the land will be fertile. But it is true. A "righteous" ruler is one who respects and cares for the people and things for which he is responsible, because he knows that God cares for and respects him. See note on "righteousness" on p. 107. Such a ruler feels responsible for the "mountains" (v. 3) and "the land" (v. 16) with the result that crops are made to grow even on the high land (v. 16b).

In modern times many rulers have lost this care and respect for the land. Some rulers, for instance, have allowed tens of thousands of trees to be cut down, some of which have taken 100 years or 500 years to grow. This is in order to make money quickly for their country. But in many cases they have done this without planting new young trees to replace those cut down. The result is that the wind blows away the top-soil, and leaves behind soil which is too poor to produce crops.

We certainly need "righteous" rulers in order to have fertile mountains and land.

**Ps. 72.7: May peace abound.** The Hebrew word translated "peace" is *shalom*. Many people know this word, because "Shalom" (or "Salaam", another form of the same word) is part of everyday greetings in many languages (including Aramaic which Jesus spoke). But people know less about the meaning of the word. Often it means to them only the end of fighting or the end of noise. (It does sometimes mean that in the Bible, but that is not its most important meaning.)

Writers in the Bible used the word "Shalom" in order to express the idea of "completeness". They had in mind especially the completeness which exists when different parts of a thing are working together or fitting in together, e.g. in a choir, or in a group of musicians, each of whom may watch the others (or the leader) so that the group may keep time. Throughout the Bible we find that this "completeness" or "harmony" or "order" was thought of as a gift from God.

Another psalm in which the word "shalom" is used is Psalm 29. The writer both describes the noise and violence of a thunderstorm (vv. 3–9), and also praises God for His "peace" (vv. 1 and 2, 10 and 11). But the writer is not saying that God brought peace after the storm. The truth is that God holds together both the storm and His People in one order. This "holding together" is the "shalom" He gives.

There are five sorts of completeness or *shalom* according to the writers in the Bible:

1. Completeness in a person, when he is at peace with himself, and when the different parts of his body are working together. Such a person can sleep soundly (Ps. 4.8).

2. Completeness in a person's circumstances. "The Lord makes peace . . . he fills you with the finest of the wheat" (Ps. 147.14). And see Psalm 72.3 (RSV) where *shalom* is translated "prosperity".

3. Completeness in a community, i.e. people being in a right relation with other people. See Hebrews 12.14 "Strive for peace with all men".

4. Completeness in a person who is in a right relation with God. This is the meaning of *shalom* in this verse.

5. Completeness in a person who is in a right relation with God because Jesus Christ has made this possible. This is of course the way in which New Testament writers use it. "We have peace with God through our Lord Jesus Christ" (Rom. 5.1).

**Ps. 72.8: May he have dominion from sea to sea.** This is not simply a prayer that the ruler will overcome other nations. The Israelite king was the representative of God. If he conquered a tribe, then that tribe would become subject to God as well as subject to the Israelites. So this is a prayer that more and more of God's human family may obey Him.

Nevertheless it was easy for an Israelite ruler to want to conquer other people for the wrong reason, e.g. in order to make a name for himself or to increase his wealth. This happened often according to the Old Testament, and it is the reason why the prophets would not allow the army to take "booty" (see Hab. 2.8, 9). And it still happens. Powerful nations subdue less powerful nations, saying that they are "liberating" them, while really they are overcoming them for their own gain.

Unfortunately Christians sometimes do this too. They may force their opinions or rules on other Christians (or on people of other religions) who are too weak to resist. They sincerely believe that by their actions the dominion of God may be more widely spread. But it may be that the real reason is to increase their own dominion rather than God's. **Ps. 72.10b: May the kings of Sheba and Seba bring gifts.** Some people, when they read this verse, remember the story of the wise men who brought gifts to Jesus (Matt. 2). They ask, "Did the writer of Psalm 72 foretell that this would happen to Jesus?"

Many people say that he did foretell this and that God gave him special knowledge in order to do so. Others give a different answer. They firmly believe that God has the power to give special knowledge to people, but they point out that:

(a) It is not possible to answer the question with certainty, since we do not have enough information.

(b) We do not need to believe that God helped the writer to foretell a future event, in order to believe in God.

(c) There are no kings in St Matthew's account.

Many Christians, as they read this psalm, are content to say "Thank God for giving us a King who is much more wonderful than the writer had in mind, or than any of the Israelites expected the Messiah would be".

## STUDY SUGGESTIONS

WORDS

1. (a) Which four of the following words describe the chief meaning of the Hebrew word *shalom* ("peace"):
   inactivity   wholeness   harmony   idleness   submission   health   deadness   completeness
   (b) What word is used for "peace" in another language which you know?
   (c) What is the chief meaning given to that word by those who use it?
   (d) What thought did the writer of Psalm 29.11 have when he used the word "peace"?

CONTENT

2. What was the important truth about God which the writer of Psalm 72 recognized?
3. What is the meaning of the statement: "The People of Israel was both a State and a Church" (p. 88)?
4. (a) Why was Samuel unwilling to give the Israelites a king?
   (b) Who was the king whom he later gave them?

5. (a) In what way are vv. 12–15 of Psalm 72 like vv. 3–7?

(b) In what way are vv. 16 and 17 like v. 3?

6. (a) What is meant by "parallelism"?

(b) Give one example of parallelism from the second half of Psalm 72.

## BIBLE

7. Read the following passages and say in each case whether the writer referred to "peace" as (i) God's gift, (ii) a man's prosperity, (iii) a man in right relation with other people, (iv) a man in right relation with God, or (v) a man in right relation with God because Jesus has made it possible:

(a) Ps. 37.37    (b) Ps. 72.3a    (c) Ps. 119.165    (d) Ps. 122.8    (e) Ps. 147.14    (f) Acts 10.36    (g) 1 Cor. 14.33    (h) Gal. 1.3    (i) Phil. 4.7

8. (a) "Another Royal Psalm is Psalm 2" (p. 91). Read Psalm 2. Do you think it should be used in Christian worship today?

(b) If so, how could it be best used? Give reasons for your answer.

## DISCUSSION AND RESEARCH

9. (a) What guidance does your Church give you, or what written prayers does it provide, on the matter of praying for the leaders of the country?

(b) Comment on any written prayers that exist, and make suggestions, if you have any, for improving them.

(c) For which of the leaders do you usually pray in public worship?

(d) What help in this matter could you obtain from studying Psalm 72?

10. (a) To what different groups do you personally belong?

(b) What is the title of the head or leader of each group?

11. (a) In what ways can the leader of a country show that he is subordinate to God or to any other authority which is superior to himself?

(b) Is the leader more likely to acknowledge that he is subject to God if he joins in the public worship of religious bodies? Give reasons for your opinion.

12. "The most terrible thing that could happen to an Israelite was to be excluded from membership" (p. 88).

(a) In what circumstances, if any, should Christians exclude other Christians from their fellowship or forbid them to receive Communion with the congregation?

(b) How far does your Church follow the instructions given by St Paul in 2 Thessalonians 3.14 and 15 and 1 Corinthians 5.13?

13. Compare the modern hymn "Hail to the Lord's anointed" (the first verse is found on p. 92), with the RSV translation of Psalm 72.

Which of the two sorts of worship will be the more helpful for a congregation which you know? Give reasons for your answer, and say which congregation you have in mind.
14. Do you think that the writer of Psalm 72.10b foretold that wise men would bring gifts to the infant Jesus? Give reasons for your answer.

# The Wings that Protect
# Psalm 91

## THEME

### 1. THE EXPERIENCE: WEAKNESS

A woman talking to a neighbour says, "My children don't listen to what I say."

A man in prison tells a visitor, "I am in prison because I did not have enough money for the bribe."

An old woman sitting on a bench at the roadside beckons to a girl, "Pick up my stick, dear; I can't bend down now."

In a letter from Haiti the writer says, "How can I escape from this spell which has been placed upon me?"

A student taking an examination for the third and last time: "I've failed twice already."

A minister referring to a member of his congregation: "Whenever I meet him I say to myself 'Speak gently to him' but before five minutes have gone I have said something I regretted later."

A girl referring to her teacher and classmates: "If I say nothing they call me unco-operative, but when I do say something they laugh at me."

From a letter written to a newspaper by a West Indian born in London: "When I was a child the white people enjoyed my company, but when I wanted to get a job this came to an end. I can obtain no work now except manual work."

A newly-married wife: "I am not what my husband hoped I would be."

A member of a Church committee: "We Christians worship God every Sunday, but what use are we to the town we live in?"

It was people who felt like this who created Psalm 91. There were so many things to make them feel powerless and defenceless, and they described those things in words such as "the terror" (v. 5) and "the destruction" (v. 6). But in spite of their weakness they also recognized in faith that God was at work in them.

Two other psalms in which the writers show the same sort of "faith" in God at a time of weakness are 4 and 121.

Psalm 4 is probably the psalm of a king:

V. 1: I am in trouble (perhaps there was a rebellion).

Vv. 2–5: I give a warning to the rebels.

Vv. 6–8: I have the joy and peace which comes from trusting God whatever happens. "Joy in my heart" (v. 7). "In peace I will . . . sleep; for thou alone, O Lord, makest me dwell in safety" (v. 8).

Psalm 121 seems also to refer to a national leader.

In vv. 1 and 2 the leader says he needs help, and that he has confidence in God.

In vv. 3–8 the worshippers say, "Yes, indeed you can trust God", and they give their reasons, e.g. "He who keeps Israel will neither slumber nor sleep".

St Paul experienced something even more than this. He had found that it was *especially* at times of helplessness that he was able to let God work through him. "I will boast of my weakness, that the power of Christ may rest upon me . . . When I am weak, then I am strong" (2 Cor. 12.9, 10).

## 2. THE RECOGNITION OF GOD

We learn what the Israelites believed about God's activity from (a) the verbs in this psalm, (b) the picture-words they use for God, (c) the names they use for God.

(a) The *verbs* (twelve of them) show what they saw God doing. See especially "deliver", "protect", "be with" and "rescue" (vv. 14, 15).

(b) The *picture*-words which refer to God compare Him to a shelter or shade for travellers (v. 1), a refuge or fortress against enemies (vv. 2, 9), pinions or wings, with which a mother bird protects her chickens from a hawk (v. 4), a shield against an enemy's arrows (v. 4c), a house in which a family can feel safe and secure (v. 9).

(c) The four *names* for God, in the Hebrew, are:

*Elyon* (v. 1a) ("Most high")—a name used by the Phoenicians for a god and later used by the Canaanites at Jerusalem.

*El-Shaddai* (v. 1b) ("Almighty")—another very old name, used by Abraham and perhaps meaning "God of the mountains" (see Gen. 17.1).

*Yahweh* (v. 2) ("The Lord")—this was the name used in the southern part of the country, i.e. in Judah, for writing about God. But people regarded this name as too holy to be spoken aloud, so in speaking about God they used the word *Adonai* (i.e. "my Lord") instead. As we have seen, when an Israelite wrote the name Yahweh, he thought of the past history of his people whom God had brought from slavery in Egypt and with whom God had made His special Covenant.

*Elohim* (v. 2) (God)—a general name for God.

From these words it is clear that the Israelite worshippers looked to

God rather than to magical powers to protect them. This is the important truth.

### 3. THE RESPONSE

In Psalm 91 the response is different from the response in other psalms because it is not a prayer made to God. Its plan is:

**Vv. 1-13:** A statement, probably made by a priest, assuring the worshippers that God is trustworthy, e.g. "He will deliver you" (v. 3).

**Vv. 14-16:** A promise made in the name of God (also by a priest): "I will deliver him" (v. 14).

Although the psalm may not look like an act of worship or a response to God, yet worshippers used it in this way. Their attitude to God shows both trust and responsibility.

1. *Trust* Someone who trusts God looks away from himself to the God who is trustworthy. This is the reason why we say that the opposite of fear is not courage but trust.

When we say the Church's creed "I believe in one God . . ." we are saying what those worshippers said then. This outlook is one which many people have as children, which they often lose afterwards, and which they need later to regain in a deeper sense than before.

There are many other psalms which are prayers of confidence. We may note:

Psalm 23. "The Lord is my shepherd (v. 1). See note on p. 40.

Psalm 27. "The Lord is my light and my salvation; whom shall I fear?" (v. 1).

Psalm 31, especially vv. 1-5.

Psalm 46. "God is our refuge and strength" (v. 1).

Psalm 62. "He only is my rock and my salvation" (v. 6).

Psalm 121. "My help comes from the Lord" (v. 2).

There are many other psalms which contain verses which are prayers of trust, e.g. 22.28, 37.5, 52.8, 57.7, 61.3, 86.7, 130.5, 144.2.

The great truth in all these psalms and verses is this:

"Lord, I believe that you are good even though you often do not treat me in the way that I expect. As I commit myself whole-heartedly to you, I find the strength that holds me up in my weakness." See 1 Peter 5.6, 7.

The pilgrim monk-priest S. K. Mandal, who had worked for a long time in the city of Calcutta in India, was invited to superintend the Church in the undeveloped Santal country. In such country it was not possible to travel by car as he had been doing. He was not a young man, and was greatly afraid that his body would not be able to bear the strain of bicycling and walking through deep mud and water. But he made his plans for travelling and committed them to God. What happened surprised him. By travelling on foot or bicycle, he got plenty of exercise and became healthier than he had ever been.

2. *Responsibility* Trusting God does not mean sitting down and waiting for Hm to protect us. God expects human beings to do the "treading" and the "trampling" (v. 13). Some people feel that this responsibility is too much for them to bear; they would prefer to be left alone in peace. "What is man, that thou makest much of him?. Wilt thou not look away from me for an instant?" See Job 7.1.–20, NEB.

As we have seen, in using Psalm 8 worshippers fully accepted their responsibility for the things which God has given. It is our responsibility to work for understanding, respect, and justice between peoples, and to use our strength if we have to defend ourselves. It is our responsibility to attack the dirt which encourages disease in a house.

It is this idea of responsibility which Jesus seems to have had in mind when the tempter quoted v. 11 of Psalm 91, and told Him to jump from the top of the Temple. See Luke 4.10, 11. There is a story from India about a Hindu "holy man" and a pupil whom he was training. They were in the jungle when they saw a leopard approaching them. The pupil stood still and prayed. The holy man said "Run! Don't ask God to do for you what you can do for yourself."

## USE

1. There are two reasons for thinking that Israelite worshippers used Psalm 91 in the services of the Temple.

(a) First, because of the phrase "his wings". This is not only picture-language to express the protection which God gives. It also reminds us that when Israelite worshippers saw the wings of the cherubim on the Ark in the Temple, they remembered that God was present. See General Note A, p. 48.

(b) Secondly it seems clear that it was a priest who spoke the psalm to the people (at public worship).

2. In congregational services Christians have often used this psalm as part of evening worship. Individuals in times of great weakness have found that vv. 14–16 helped them to return to their trust in God.

## NOTES

**Ps. 91.3: The snare of the fowler.** This is one of the eight phrases in Psalm 91 which refer to evils which might overcome the worshippers. Probably the Israelites did not think only of a real hunter's trap. As in the case of the other phrases, they thought of demons or evil spirits which (they believed) brought accidents and illnesses. It was natural for them to think in this way, since they knew nothing of the bacteria, fungi, and viruses which cause disease.

What should Christians say to the millions of people who today are afraid of such spirits, e.g. who live in fear of the power of a witch to make them ill or childless? Christians should affirm that God is good and that He is stronger than any spirits. Christians do not help others by saying that such spirits do not exist. See note on Psalm 96.5.

**Ps. 91.4: He will cover you.** The important word here is "He". In many other tribes, people hoped that magical powers would protect them. Ancient amulets have been found (e.g. in Egypt) with a picture on them of a god treading on a lion, giving magic power against wild animals to the owner of the amulets. They are only one example of the "powers" on which the Israelites might have depended. Instead, they looked to God.

In some parts of the world a "doctor" sells animals' bones which people use as charms or amulets. He promises that these charms will protect the wearer against disease or even death. In other places car-drivers wear "St Christopher medals" believing that these will protect them against accidents.

The Psalms too have been used as magic. There are books in which we read, for example, that "if you stand in the running water of a river and recite Psalm 37, you will become stronger than any enemy." But God calls Christians to live in obedience to Him and to use the intelligence which he has given them instead of depending on charms.

We still need to ask what sort of protection the Israelites believed that God gave:

1. It is probable that, like the writer of Psalm 91, they really believed that God did prevent evil from coming to them when they were faithful to Him. "No evil shall befall you" (v. 10). The writer of Psalm 37.25 seems to have believed this: "I have not seen the righteous forsaken or his children begging bread". So did one of Job's friends: "Who that was innocent ever perished?" (Job. 4.7).

2. But perhaps they were simply expressing in poetry the truth that God gives protection. Perhaps they realized that believers as well as unbelievers suffer, but they also knew that God does not let the suffering be overwhelming. Julian of Norwich wrote in 1393, "He said not 'Thou shalt not be afflicted', but He said, 'Thou shalt not be overcome'."

Whichever answer the writers of Psalm 91 had in mind, Christians give the second answer. What St Paul said about God's help in times of temptation is also true about His help in times of suffering: "God keeps faith and He will not allow you to be tested above your powers, but when the test comes He will at the same time provide a way out, by enabling you to sustain it" (1 Cor. 10.13, NEB). When we are weak, God delivers us, not from all pain but from despair and from isolation. What God gives us may be rescue *out of* trouble or it may be support *in* trouble: "I will be with him in trouble" (Ps. 91.15).

"I have the joy and peace which comes from trusting God whatever happens" (p. 98).

Nigerian travellers—like railway passengers anywhere—trust their lives to those who made the carriages and those who drive the train.

What exactly is "trust"?

An experienced teacher in Uganda believed that God was calling him to be trained as a minister. During his time at the Theological School he received an allowance which was only half the amount of his salary as a teacher. He and his wife had nine children and they had to pay school fees for four of them. After one month the Church had to reduce his allowance. A year later this allowance was halved owing to drought in the area from which the money was collected. When a friend asked him why he continued his training, he said, "God has brought us here, and He will see us through."

**Ps. 91.7: A thousand may fall . . . but it will not come near you.** We have seen above that the writer probably did mean that anyone who was faithful to God would escape suffering. It may therefore be useful to note briefly four stages in the thinking of the Israelites about suffering. (The writer of Psalm 91 probably belonged to Stage 3.)

Stage 1: (Before the Israelite Patriarchs, i.e. before 1400 BC):
"You cannot rely on the gods. They send pain or pleasure as they like. It is all a matter of chance."

Stage 2: (Between 1400 BC and the Exile into Babylon):
"God is just. If we Israelites are faithful to Him as a People, He will protect us as a People."

Stage 3: (After the Exile, i.e. after 500 BC):
"God is just. I belong to the People of God and if I keep the law, God will protect me personally."

Stage 4: (The Book of Job):
"Even if I keep the law, I may still suffer. Yet I believe that God is just." See notes on Psalms 22.7 and 51.8.

**Ps. 91.8: The recompense of the wicked,** i.e. the punishment which God will give to the wicked. We who read this, use the word "wicked" to mean someone whose behaviour is bad. The Hebrew word *rasha* used in this verse does mean this, but the Israelites very often used it in a different way. See note on Ps. 139.24. The following is an outline of the ideas which they probably held when they used the word. (The outline is true also of other Hebrew words which are translated in English by such words as "sinners", "enemies".)

1. The world would be in disorder if it had not been for God who created order. "The earth was without form" (Gen. 1.2).

2. This God made us Israelites His People by the Covenant. "Behold the blood of the covenant which the Lord has made with you" (Exod. 24.8).

3. There are other people who are outside the Covenant, and because they are outside it they are against order in the world.

4. They show this by practising magic and behaving as if there was no God. "All his thoughts are, 'There is no God'" (Ps. 10.4).

5. God will not allow these "outsiders" to be successful. "You will see the recompense of the wicked" (Ps. 91.8).

6. God's enemies are our enemies. Therefore we join with God and fight them. "Do not I hate them that hate thee . . ." (Ps. 139.21).

7. Some of these enemies are not "outsiders", but Israelites who break the Covenant and practise magic or worship other gods.

See also note on p. 74.

**Ps. 91.14b: He knows my name.** In this verse "he" refers to anyone who puts his confidence in God. Such people know enough about God to be able to trust Him completely. "Name" means "character" or "personality". See note on Psalm 8.1a.

## STUDY SUGGESTIONS

### WORDS

1. What are the twelve English verbs or verbal phrases in the RSV translation of Psalm 91 which describe what God does for people in trouble?

2. What seven words did the writers of Psalm 91.1–10 use to describe the things that made them feel weak and powerless?

3. "Their attitude to God shows trust" (p. 99). Give three other English words which have the same meaning as "trust".

### CONTENT

4. What are the four names for God which the writer of Psalm 91 used? (Give the English translations.)

5. Are the following statements true or untrue? Give reasons for your answer in each case:

(i) If a man is faithful to God, that man will not suffer.

(ii) If a man trusts God to protect him, he is still responsible for protecting himself.

(iii) Israelites thought of the people of other nations as "wicked".

### BIBLE

6. Rewrite Psalm 91.14–16 in the form of a prayer to God, e.g. "Because I cleave to You in love, You will deliver me . . .".

7. "Two other psalms in which writers show the same sort of faith in God at a time of weakness are Psalms 4 and 121" (p. 97).

Read these two psalms and say in each case:

(a) What phrase shows the distress of the writer?

(b) What phrase shows his faith?

8. Compare the following passages with Psalm 91, and say in each case in what way the thought is like the thought of Psalm 91:

(a) Rom. 8.35–39  (b) 1 Cor. 10.9–13  (c) 2 Cor. 12.9–10

9. (a) What do the following passages all refer to:

(b) What is the truth about God which all the passages contain?

(c) How useful is it to use this sort of language today in order to point to that truth about God? Give reasons for your answer.
Gen. 24.7; Ps. 91.11; Dan. 3.28; Matt. 18.10

DISCUSSION AND RESEARCH

10. What would you reply to a friend who said that Christians should not use Psalm 91.8 in worship, because it reminds them of their hatred of their unfriendly neighbours and stirs up enmity against people of other nations?

11. "Israelite worshippers looked to God, rather than to magical powers", to protect them (p. 98).
(a) Give two examples from everyday life of people entrusting themselves to other powers or things *rather than* trusting God.
(b) Give two examples of people entrusting themselves to other powers or things *as well as* trusting God.

12. The saying of St Paul "When I am weak then I am strong" (2 Cor. 12.10) is quoted on p. 98.
(a) Explain briefly what Paul meant.
(b) Give an example from your own experience, or from the experience of someone whom you know, of the truth of this.

13. Which verse in Psalm 91 would you choose to use as a chorus verse? (It should contain the main thought of the psalm.) Give reasons for your choice.

14. "A thousand may fall but it will not come near you" (Ps. 91.7). An American mother and her children were living in Cambodia when the war spread into that country. Each evening the small town where they were living was bombed. One night an English woman came to sleep with the family. She said the next day, "This is the first night I have felt calm enough to sleep. I knew I should be all right sleeping with you because you go to Church."
Comment on the attitude and belief of that English woman.

# A New Song
# Psalm 96

## THEME

### 1. THE EXPERIENCE: BELONGING TO THE HUMAN RACE

The Russian writer, Yevtushenko, has told how in 1941 when he was a boy, he saw 20,000 war prisoners marching through Moscow. They were German soldiers captured while they were invading Russia. The crowd who watched was mainly of women, and nearly every woman had had a relative killed by the Germans. At first the women stared at the soldiers with hatred, and would have attacked them if the police had not prevented them. Then as the thousands of these bloodstained, wounded Germans marched by, a change took place. The women began to feel compassion. Then one woman crawled through the line of policemen, went up to a German soldier, and pushed half a loaf of black bread into his pocket. Yevtushenko wrote, "Now suddenly from every side women were running towards the soldiers, pushing into their hands bread, cigarettes, whatever they had. The soldiers were no longer enemies. They were people."

Some members of staff at Makerere University College, Uganda (a Ugandan, a Pole, an Indian, and an Englishman) were listening to the news on the radio. It was at the time when the Russians had put atomic rockets on Cuba, which were powerful enough to destroy American cities. The President of USA had said that if the Russians did not remove the rockets, the USA would attack Russia with atomic weapons. The Indian said, "Mankind will live or die in the next twenty-four hours." He meant that if USA fired their atomic weapons, not only parts of Russia and USA would be destroyed, but that all human beings would be affected.

During the Vietnam war, Viet Cong soldiers arrested a group of newspaper reporters whom they found in the jungle. The reporters were a Japanese, a Chinese, and an Australian girl. As the soldiers could not understand what the reporters were saying, it seemed likely for many days that the soldiers would think they were enemies and kill them. The Australian wrote, "The differences between our nationalities became unimportant. We were simply three human beings, cheering each other up and desperately hoping we were going to live."

So in different ways people experience that there is such a thing as "mankind", and that they belong to it. Differences between families or tribes or nations are real and important, but the larger family which is the whole "human race" or "mankind" also is real. As John Donne (1573–1631) said, in a sermon, "No man is an *Island*, . . . every man is a piece of the continent, a part of the main; . . . any man's *death* diminishes *me*, because I am involved in *Mankind*."

The Israelites who used Psalm 96 in their worship had in some way had this experience. We notice such phrases as the following, "all the earth" (vv. 1, 9, 13), "the peoples" (vv. 3, 5, 7, 10, 13), "the nations" (vv. 3, 10). Of course the worshippers could not know about all the inhabitants of the world. They only knew about those who lived in Mediterranean or Western Asian countries. But they did know something which many people today do not yet know: that there is one God who is Creator and King of mankind and of all nature. In this connection see also Psalm 46, one of the "Hymns of Zion". It is also a prayer of confidence in God, as we see from the chorus verse (v. 7 and v. 11): "The Lord of hosts is with us; the God of Jacob is our refuge." But here we notice especially v. 10, "Be still and know that I am God: I am exalted among the nations", i.e. God whom the worshippers honour as their King (perhaps at a New Year Festival) is King of all mankind.

## 2. THE RECOGNITION OF GOD

In Psalm 96 the words "save", "make", "reign", "judge", "righteous", and "true" (which are often used in other psalms too) show us what the Israelites believed about God.

1. He *saves* (v. 2). See notes on Psalm 22.21 and Psalm 67.2.

2. He *makes* (v. 5). The Israelites thought of God as the maker of the world in times past. "He made us" (Ps. 100.3). They also recognized Him as the continual creator and sustainer. "Thou renewest the face of the ground" (Ps. 104.30). See note on Psalm 100.3b.

3. He *reigns* (v. 10). The Israelites said three things about God's reigning:

(a) He has defeated the forces of chaos and has established order. He is therefore king over the whole universe. "His kingdom rules over all" (Ps. 103.19b).

(b) He rules over all human rulers and controls them. Rulers and their peoples may rebel against God, but God remains King. "Say among the nations 'The Lord reigns'"(Ps. 96.10).

(c) God's sovereignty is partly seen now. There will come a time when it will be fully seen. See note on Psalm 96.13.

4. He *judges* (vv. 10, 13). As we have seen the Israelites were happy, not frightened, to know that God "judged". See note on Psalm 19.9. It meant that there was justice and order in the world, and that people were not simply under the control of "luck" or "fate". Note especially that:

(a) He judges righteously (vv. 10, 13). When the Israelites called God "righteous", they were saying two things:

(i) That God loves human beings, that He rescues from the power of evil those who are doing wrong, and gives strength and comfort to those who are suffering. "Gracious is the Lord and righteous: our God is merciful" (Ps. 116.5).

(ii) That God shares His righteousness with human beings. "Give ... thy righteousness to the royal son" (Ps. 72.1). So a "righteous" person is one who allows God to work in him in this way, i.e. one who has a loving concern for other people.

(b) He judges with truth (v. 13). When they said that God was "true" they meant that He was always trustworthy. See note on p. 52.

Those worshippers recognized God in so many ways that it is not surprising that they made such a vigorous response to Him.

"Sing to the Lord, all the earth" (Ps. 96.1)—young and old, male and female, dark and light, from Britain to Brazil, the Pacific to Pakistan, from Egypt to Japan.

## 3. THE RESPONSE

We see how the worshippers responded to God from the words in the psalm which show what they did, e.g. sing (v. 1), bless (v. 2), tell (v. 2), declare (v. 3), ascribe to, i.e. acknowledge and recognize, (v. 7). They felt that it was important to express outwardly what they believed inwardly about God's activity.

There are four parts in Psalm 96:

**Vv. 1–3:** The opening call to all Israelites to come and praise God.

**Vv. 4–6:** The central act of praise, in which the worshippers say why they are praising God.

**Vv. 7–9** A second call, addressed to all human beings, to worship God.

**Vv. 10–13:** A third call, addressed to all created things, to worship their Creator.

## USE

Many scholars think that the Israelites used this psalm at an annual festival of which we read in 1 Kings 8.2. "The feast in the month Ethanim, which is the seventh month." At this autumn festival they remembered the Covenant which God had made with them, and the care which He had shown to them over many years. It took place at harvest time. Thus it was a sort of New Year Festival. See General Note A, p. 46.

During this festival there seems to have been a special ceremony in which worshippers "enthroned" God as King and Creator. "The Lord reigns!" (v. 10). They "enthroned" Him by carrying the wooden Ark in procession, see Psalm 47.5: "God has gone up with a shout!" The winged figures of the cherubim were the sign of the presence of God. As the procession continued there was music and shouting and singing (vv. 1, 2), some worshippers prostrated themselves on the ground (v. 9b), others danced, and sacrifices were offered (v. 8b).

Another psalm which worshippers probably used at this festival is Psalm 93. The first words "The Lord reigns" do not mean that God has just begun to reign. They mean "We once again recognize that God is in control of our world." In vv. 3 and 4 we note that flood and sea-water were symbols of everything that seems to be disorderly and without meaning. But God is "mightier" (v. 4).

Other psalms which many scholars call "Enthronement Psalms" are: 47, 95, 97–100.

## NOTES

**Ps. 96.1: A new song.** Worshippers called Psalm 96 a "new" song because the festival was a renewing for them in three ways:

(a) They renewed their loyalty to God to whom they belonged through the Covenant;

(b) They renewed their sure belief that God had overcome the power of chaos and was King over all mankind and all creation;

(c) They celebrated the harvest, which was a sign of the new life which God continued to give to His peoples.

The words point to a truth about God and a truth about people who are obedient to Him:

1. God creates changes in the world. "Behold, the former things have come to pass and new things I now declare . . . Sing to the Lord a new song" (Isa. 42.9, 10). People do not live under "Fate", but under God who does unexpected things because He loves people. See note on p. 138.

During the 1967–70 civil war in Nigeria between the "Federal" army (West and North) and the "Biafran" army (from the East), a group of badly wounded men from the West found that this was true. They had been taken to a hospital in the "enemy" area of Biafra, and were afraid that they would be shot or simply left to die. But a courageous Biafran nursing sister said, "We must treat these patients first even though they are Federals. Their condition is far worse than the condition of our own soldiers."

When the war was over there were many signs of God creating changes which surprised people. One day the bishops of a Church in the East of Nigeria received an unexpected deputation of Church leaders from the West. These leaders from the West had come with £1,000, and they explained that it was the first part of a present to help to rebuild churches and schools in the East. As one bishop said at the time, "God is always at work in His world".

2. People are obedient to God when they are open to His will to create change. Sometimes Christians are open to His will by co-operating with others who are already working for necessary changes. In many parts of South America, for instance, Christians are working with Communists to get changes made in the laws about the rents which landlords charge very poor people.

Sometimes Christians are the first to work for such changes. In many countries they have been the first to work for the health and welfare of very poor people, because God in Jesus Christ showed that He was concerned for the welfare of everyone. They have often done this against the customs of their country, e.g. when they saved twins instead of destroying them. In other countries it is due to the work of Christians that girls are admitted to schools, and that women are becoming partners of their husbands rather than their servants in a marriage.

At other times Christians change the ways in which they themselves do things, e.g. Roman Catholics at the Vatican Council in 1964–5 believed that God was wanting them to change some of the ways in which they had worshipped for many hundreds of years.

**Ps. 96.3: Among the nations.** There were three different ways in which the Israelites regarded other nations:

1. The way of *unity*. The Israelites felt that they themselves and other nations both had the same Lord and Creator. This is one of the ways in which the writer of Psalm 96 spoke of "the nations". See note on p. 52.

2. The way of *separation*. The Israelites knew that they were different from other nations, and described the others as "enemies", "wicked", "heathen", "idolaters" because they served other gods. This is another way in which the writer of Psalm 96 thought of "the nations". "The gods of the peoples are idols" (v. 5). See note on Psalm 67.2b.

3. The way of *responsibility*. The Israelites believed that they were responsible for giving other nations knowledge of God, i.e. that others would receive God's blessing and the full truth about Him through the Israelites. "In you all the families of the earth will be blessed" (Gen. 12.3, RSV marginal note).

When Jesus came, Simeon called Him "a light for revelation to the Gentiles" (Luke 2.32). And Jesus Himself told His followers to share with people of all nations what He had shown them about God's love.

Christians have regarded people of other religions in different ways.

(a) Some have kept themselves apart from other people. There was hardly one Christian who travelled to Muslim countries between the death of Muhammad in AD 632 and the visit of St Francis to the Sultan of Egypt in 1219.

(b) Others have feared or despised them as enemies. "Muslims are irreclaimable enemies," said Luther in the sixteenth century.

(c) Some have worked with them as partners in the fight against evil. "Cuscon", the Calcutta Urban Service Consortium, is a body which organizes relief after riots and floods, as well as undertaking many other sorts of service in the city. In this work Christians join with Hindus, Muslims, and other groups.

(d) And some have been true to the commands of Christ and served the people of other religions in love. Some do it as individuals, like the many nurses and doctors from Africa, Asia, and the Caribbean who are staffing hospitals in the West, or like technicians, teachers, and missionaries who have gone to share their knowledge with the peoples of developing nations. Others serve in such groups as Christian Aid or Cafod, or the various United Nations organizations.

**Ps. 96.5: All the gods of the peoples are idols.**

1. What is meant by "gods"?

(a) People speak about "gods" when they are thinking about unseen powers which (they believe) can either help them or injure them. It is therefore dangerous not to pay attention to these "gods". People believed this at the time when the Psalms were written, and people believe it today in very many parts of the world.

(b) The "power" who is served, or "worshipped", is sometimes thought of as a tribal hero who has died. Sometimes it is the spirit of a thing or an event, e.g. of storms or childbirth or the earth. (Many Yorubas in West Africa serve Shango who is both a past hero, and, they believe, the spirit behind thunderstorms.) Sometimes it is the spirit of an ancestor.

(c) People often believe that a spirit has its own territory, just as David believed that God could only be worshipped in the land round Jerusalem. When David had been driven out by Saul he said that he would have to serve "other gods", i.e. the gods of the wilderness where he and his followers were encamped (1 Sam. 26.19). Thus very many people serve a "spirit" or "god" whom they believe to be connected with one special tree or mountain or forest or river or lake.

(d) People sometimes make "idols" or images to represent the gods or spirits whom they serve. They believe that the idol contains the power of the god, or even that the god actually "lives" in the idol. After a time people may come to believe that the image itself has power which can be used to change the course of events, either to gain prosperity or against enemies.

2. What did the Israelites believe about these "gods"?

(a) At first they thought that these gods were real and powerful, but less powerful than the God of Israel. "The Lord is a great king above all gods" (Ps. 95.3).

(b) Israelites were often tempted to serve these "other gods", and often did so. But they knew that they owed loyalty to the God who had made a special Covenant with them. "You shall have no other gods before me" (Exod. 20.3).

(c) Later they believed that other gods had no real existence. "Before me no god was formed, nor shall there be any after me" (Isa. 43.10). See also Isaiah 44.9–17. It is not certain whether the writer of Psalm 96 believed that the gods of other nations did not exist at all or that they were gods without power. (The word "idols" in v. 5 means "nothings", or "powerless spirits"; it does not mean things made of wood or stone.)

3. Do these "other gods" or "spirits" exist? There are different answers which Christians give, of which the following are two:

(a) That such "gods" or "spirits" do exist, both good and evil; and that St Paul referred to evil ones in Eph. 6.12 "the spiritual hosts of wickedness".

(b) That "other gods" and "spirits" do not exist, but that human beings make things and people into "gods" by treating them as supremely important. Some people show, by the way they behave, that they have put the State in the place of the true God: they have made it a "god". Others make their family into a "god". Others show, by the time which they spend on looking after their possessions, that for them their possessions are "gods". What we believe about "other gods" clearly affects the way we live.

We may notice here another psalm in which the word "gods" is used, Psalm 97. This is another "Enthronement Psalm". Its plan is:

Vv. 1–5: God is in control of His creation and of all evil.
Vv. 6–9: God is in control of all other "gods". "All gods bow down before him" (v. 7). "Thou art exalted far above all gods" (v. 9).
Vv. 10–12: God gives power and joy to those who go on "hating evil" (v. 10).

**Ps. 96.8: Bring an offering.** At some point in the Temple worship, the animals which the worshippers had brought as their "offerings" were sacrificed.

Sometimes a sacrifice was a sign of thanksgiving to God, and of dependence on Him. "Offer to God a sacrifice of thanksgiving" (Ps. 50.14).

Sometimes the worshippers offered it in order that God might remove their guilt. "It is the blood that makes atonement" (Lev. 17.11).

But usually sacrifice was a sign of the fellowship that worshippers had with God. Part of the animal was eaten, so that the sacrifice became a fellowship-meal.

In the New Testament, writers taught that the living and dying and rising of Christ had been a sort of sacrifice. The writer to the Hebrews added that Christ had done more for human beings than had ever been done through the old sacrifices. "He has appeared once for all at the end of the age to put away sin by the sacrifice of himself" (Heb. 9.26).

Christians "bring their offerings" in many different ways: by actively serving their fellow human-beings ("Present your bodies as a living sacrifice", Romans 12.1); by worshipping God ("offer up a sacrifice of praise", Hebrews 13.15); by sharing their possessions with others ("The gifts you sent . . . a sacrifice acceptable to God", Philippians 4.18); by dying if necessary for Christ's sake ("I am already on the point of being sacrificed", 2 Timothy 4.6). In these and other ways they join their "offering" with the offering which Christ made "once for all".

**Ps. 96.10: The Lord reigns . . . He will judge.** As we have seen (p. 107) Psalm 96 is one of several psalms in which the worshippers think of God as "King". In this verse they also think of Him as "Judge". Both these words are only picture-words.

Such words are necessary because we cannot help using some words in order to talk about God. But they are always dangerous, because they say less than the truth about Him. E.g. there is some truth in calling God "King" or "Judge", but in some ways these words give an untrue picture of Him. See note on p. 126.

**Ps. 96.13: He comes . . . He will judge the world.** We saw that those who first used this psalm had had the experience of belonging to the whole human race. In this verse they looked forward to the time when the whole human race, the "world", would recognize God as King. They praised Him as being King already, but they also believed that at some future time all the world would know for certain that He was King. See note on Psalm 98.9.

## STUDY SUGGESTIONS

WORDS

1. What *ten* words or phrases in vv. 1–10 of Psalm 96 refer to the activity of the worshippers? (One example is "tell' (v. 2b).)

CONTENT

2. Worshippers probably sang Psalm 96 at an Enthronement Festival (p. 109).
   (a) Whom were they "enthroning"?
   (b) What did they do to show that an "enthronement" was taking place?
3. At what time of year did the festival take place at which Psalm 96 was sung?
4. What *two* words or phrases used in Psalm 96 show what sort of judgement God gives?
5. (a) Give *two* reasons why the Israelites made sacrifices as part of their worship.
   (b) Which verse in Psalm 96 refers to sacrifice?

BIBLE

6. (a) What phrase do all the following passages from the Psalms contain?
   33.3; 40.3; 98.1; 144.9 149.1
   (b) Why did the writers of these psalms use this phrase?
7. "Other psalms which the Israelites used at this sort of Enthronement Festival are 47, 93, 95, 97–100" (p. 109). Choose two sentences from each of these psalms which suggest that worshippers used them at this Festival.
8. Read the following passages and say in each case whether the writer is saying:
   (i) That other gods do not exist.

114

(ii) That other gods are inferior to the One True God.
(a) Deut. 6.13–15 (b) Isa. 37.19 (c) Isa. 46. 5–9 (d) Ps. 86.8
(e) Ps. 97.7 (f) Ps. 135.5 (g) Acts 19.26 (h) Gal. 4.8

9. Concerning other nations, the Israelites felt either:
   (i) That they had unity with them under one Creator, or
   (ii) That they were separated from them, or
   (iii) That they were responsible for giving them a knowledge of
   God. Read the following passages and say in each case which of
   these three the writer had in mind:
   (a) Gen. 22.15–18 (b) Isa. 2.3 (c) Isa. 40.28 (d) Isa. 49.6
   (e) Ps. 2.1 (f) Ps. 22.27, 28 (g) Ps. 47.3 (h) Ps. 93.1 (i) Ps.
   115.2–4 (j) Zech. 8.23

DISCUSSION AND RESEARCH

10. "In different ways people experience that there is such a thing as
    mankind and that they belong to it. Differences between families
    and tribes are real. But mankind also is real." (p. 106)
    (a) Describe any experience which you yourself have had of
    belonging to the human race.
    (b) In July 1969 the American astronaut, Neil Armstrong, stepped
    on to the surface of the moon. He was the first man who did so.
    As he put his foot down he said, "One small step for a man, one
    giant leap for mankind."
    (i) What did he mean?
    (ii) What is your opinion?

11. "It was important to those worshippers that they should express
    outwardly what they inwardly believed" (p. 109).
    (a) For whose sake does a Christian worshipper outwardly express
    his belief about God: for God's, for his own, for his fellow-
    worshippers', or for people who do not worship with him? Give
    reasons for your answer.
    (b) What "outward expressions" does your Church use in its
    regular worship which the Israelites did *not* use?

12. "Sometimes Christians co-operate with others who are already
    working for necessary changes. . . . Sometimes Christians are the
    first to work for such changes." (p. 110)
    From your knowledge of the Church today give examples of
    Christians doing each of these things.

13. (a) Do you believe that "other gods" (Ps. 96.5) exist? Give your
    reasons.
    (b) What difference does it make whether a person serves "other
    gods" or not? Give examples from everyday life.

14. Which verse in Ps. 96 would you choose to use as a chorus verse?
    Give reasons for your choice.

15. "There is some truth in calling God 'King' or 'Judge', but in some ways these words give an untrue picture of Him" (p. 114).
    (a) What truth and what untruth is there in calling God (i) King? (ii) Judge?
    (b) Give another picture word used in speaking about God, and say in what ways it can be true and can be untrue.
16. "'He comes . . . He will judge the world with righteousness' (Ps. 96.13). In times of suffering Christians renew their trust in God with the help of words like these."
    What would you say to someone who complained that Christians who say this become weak, not strong, "because they expect God to protect them from evil, and wait for Him to put things right in the future, instead of working to put them right themselves"?

# General Note B
# The Psalms are for Singing
# Example, Psalm 98

## A. THE ISRAELITES SANG THE PSALMS

There are so many references to "singing" in the Psalms that it is clear that the worshippers sang rather than spoke the Psalms. "O come, let us sing to the Lord; let us make a joyful noise . . ." (Ps. 95.1). "Serve the Lord with gladness! Come into his presence with singing!" (Ps. 100.2). Some of the Hebrew verbs which are translated "sing" also mean "shout for joy" or "cry aloud" so we cannot be sure whether the Israelite worshippers actually sang, or whether they simply shouted.

*Who* did the "singing" or shouting?

Sometimes it was the whole congregation, sometimes it was the choir of priests and Levites. When a choir sang, they probably sang the verses, and the people answered by repeating a "chorus verse" (see note on p. 119) or by simply shouting "Alleluia!". But even when a choir did most of the singing, the rest of the people knew what was being sung. They could all join in the worship. "Let us exalt His Name *together*" (Ps. 34.3).

*Why* did they sing rather than speak?

First, because singing is a way by which people can show their deepest feelings as they worship God. Songs and psalms and hymns are a necessity, not a luxury, for worshippers. Secondly, the Israelites sang because, as they did so, they became united.

*When* did they sing?

We cannot answer this with certainty. But it is known that there were special events in the Temple services at which the worshippers sang, e.g. during processions, at the moment when they saw the Ark of the Covenant, and when the priests performed a sacrifice.

B. They sang to musical instruments

The Israelites used a great many musical instruments in their national life. Five different instruments were played in the Temple when psalms were sung:

*Cymbals.* One kind was called a *tsel-tsel*, and the name shows what sort of sound it made when the two brass plates were clapped together. See Psalm 150.5 and Ezra 3.10. In the case of some cymbals, the player brought one down on top of the other; with others the cymbals were brought together from the sides.

*Large harp*, called the *kinnor*, whose strings were plucked. It is sometimes translated as "lyre". There were always nine of these in the Temple. There could be any number of strings, from three to twelve.

*Small harp.* This was called a *nebel*, which is often translated "lute" or "psaltery". Two could be played together.

*Trumpet.* This was made of metal. It was long and straight and gave a high note when it was blown. In the Temple at Jerusalem there were 120 of them and they were usually blown by the priests themselves. Two were often used together (see Num. 10.2).

*Horn*, called *shofar* in Hebrew, and also translated "cornet" or "trumpet" or "shawn". It was made of the horn of a ram or of an antelope, and gave two notes.

See 1 Chronicles 15.28, "All Israel brought up the ark of the covenant of the Lord with shouting, to the sound of the horn (*shofar*), trumpets, and cymbals, and made loud music on harps (*nebel*) and lyres (*kinnor*)."

The Levites were responsible for providing music for the psalms, and they chiefly used the large harp, small harp, and the horn. But others also played these instruments.

The singing was often led by the same people who played the instruments.

C. Christians sing the Psalms

Many Christians find that it is best to sing to the glory of God in the spirit of the Psalms, rather than using the actual words of the Psalms. They create new psalms in the spirit of those who created the 150 Psalms in the Bible. This means that their "new psalms":

(a) Arise out of an actual situation which people are experiencing at the time;

(b) Point to the activity of God in that situation (in the light of their knowledge that God's activity was fully seen in Christ);

(c) Provide a response to God, in which worshippers can express themselves fully, in singing and in movement.

(d) Let all the worshippers take part, rather than leaving activity to a choir.

In this way they are singing "in the spirit of" the first psalm writers.

But Jesus himself used the actual words of the Old Testament Psalms, and for this reason and for other reasons also, many Christian congregations want to sing those words. How best can they do so?

There are five chief ways:

1. *"Metrical" Psalms*, a "direct" way of singing, i.e. a way by which the whole congregation sings the whole psalm together.

At the Reformation in the 16th century AD, the reformers aimed to help people to have a faith of their own rather than to pay priests to approach God on their behalf. They therefore provided ways in which the people could join fully in public worship. They translated the Psalms in such a way that the words were easy to memorize and each verse could be sung to the same simple tune. The metre was regular and the lines of the verse rhymed. This was especially done in France and Scotland. Here is an example of one verse from Psalm 100:

> All people that on earth do dwell,
> Sing to the Lord with cheerful voice;
> Him serve with mirth, his praise forth tell,
> Come ye before him and rejoice.

2. *Hymns based on psalms*, another "direct" way.

These hymns are unlike Metrical Psalms because they are not translations. They keep close to the psalm, but they paraphrase and interpret it. Examples of this in English are: "O God our help in ages past", which should be compared to Psalm 90, on which it is based; and "The King of love my Shepherd is" which should be compared to Psalm 23 on which it is based.

In some languages this is the best way of singing the Psalms. See one example of this on p. 121, a Hindi Hymn (from India) based on Psalm 23.

3. *"Plain-song"*: a third "direct" way of singing.

In "plain-song" the people recite the words in unison. They use only a few notes and follow the rhythm of the spoken language. Those who use this method have to learn to fit the words to the tune, so that this way is most suitable for people who worship together often (e.g. in a monastery or a school).

One of the different sorts of "plain-song" in the sixth century was "Gregorian". A thousand years later musicians composed harmonies for Gregorian chants and it was from these that the "Anglican Chant" came.

4. *The "Sharing" or "Alternating" way.*

The choir leader sings or says one verse, or the first half of a verse, and the people answer with the next verse, or the second half of the same verse.

Another way is for half the congregation to sing or say one verse or half-verse and for the other half to sing the next.

5. *The "Chorus" way*.

The leader or a small group of singers sings or says the verses, and the people sing the "chorus verse". This chorus verse is one which has been chosen from the psalm because it contains the chief thought of the psalm. Sometimes this chorus is just "Alleluia", "Praise the Lord". The Grail version of Psalm 100 is as follows

People: Alleluia, alleluia, alleluia.
Leader: Cry out with joy to the Lord, all the earth.
Serve the Lord with gladness,
Come before him, singing for joy.
People: Alleluia (3 times).
Leader: Know that he, the Lord, is God.
He made us, we belong to Him,
We are his people, the sheep of his flock.
People: Alleluia (3 times).
Leader: Go within his gate, giving thanks.
Enter his courts with songs of praise,
Give thanks to him and bless his name.
People: Alleluia (3 times).
Leader: Indeed how good is the Lord,
Eternal his merciful love;
He is faithful from age to age.
People: Alleluia (3 times).
Leader: Give glory to the Father Almighty,
To his Son, Jesus Christ our Lord,
To the Spirit that dwells in our hearts.
People: Alleluia (3 times).

We notice that the last verse is a "doxology", the verse that Christians add to every psalm to show that the psalm is being interpreted in a Christian way.

In the case of longer psalms, the leader sings two or three verses together. If the people sang the chorus after every verse, it would take too long. When the Psalms were written in Hebrew, each was often divided up into a few large paragraphs or "strophes". They were not divided into the many short verses which we know today.

There are several psalms in which it is easy to pick out the chorus verse, e.g. in Psalm 136 the chorus is placed as the second half of each verse, "For his steadfast love endures for ever." See also Psalm 8, where the chorus is vv. 1 and 9.

When the Psalms became the hymn book of the Christian Church this "chorus" way of singing them was even more used than it had been in the Temple. St Augustine, for example, knew no other way of singing the Psalms.

Today, as Christians in many countries are working to let worship be an act of the whole congregation, this way is being more and more used.

This way of singing the Psalms has many advantages:

(a) It is a way of singing which is already familiar to many people. All over the world there are traditional songs—national songs, war songs, love songs, drinking songs, work songs—which are sung by one singer, and the people sing a chorus at intervals. Today many groups of young people are singing this sort of song, often in order to protest against some evil in their country.

(b) The chorus is easy to learn. Everyone can take part, including strangers and the very young and the very old.

*Note:* It is best if the chorus is short. If it is long, it is usually divided into two parts. Some of the congregation sing one part, the others sing the other part. (See Psalm 121 below.)

(c) The chorus verse reminds the people of the chief thought of the psalm. Thus everyone can join in the worship in heart and mind as well as voice. (Some Church authorities have issued an arrangement of the Psalms, showing how each psalm can be divided up and which verse should be the chorus.)

(d) The method is suitable for all languages, including those which are "tonal", e.g. Chinese and many African languages.

For example, the arrangement of Psalm 24.1–4 shown on p. 122 was made by a student at a Uganda Theological College who had become interested in the Psalms. When it was used in the college chapel, the congregation of staff and students and their families joined vigorously in the Alleluias. The musical instruments used were a drum, a kind of cymbals, and a stringed instrument.

The arrangement of Ps. 121 which appears on p. 123 is in Tamil (a language of South India). There are three parts, which are sung by a soloist or choir: (1) vv. 3 and 4, (2) vv. 5 and 6, (3) vv. 7 and 8. Only Part 1 is given here. The congregation sings the chorus after each part, using the same tune as the soloist. The chorus is v. 1, then v. 2, then v. 1 again.

On p. 124 is an English version of Psalm 136, vv. 1–9 and 24–26. This is a part of the psalm as arranged by the Grail (see p. 124). In this version a soloist or choir sings the psalm line by line. After each line the congregation sings the chorus: "Great is His love, love without end" (see v. 1b, 2b, etc.).

## Psalm 23 lyric form in Hindi

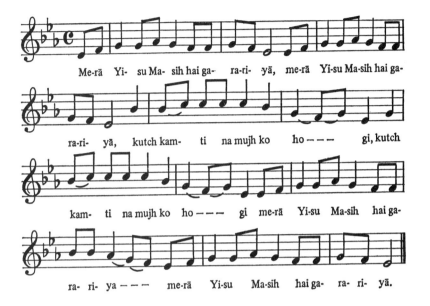

Me-rā Yi- su Ma- sih hai ga-- ra-ri- yā, me-rā Yi-su Ma-sih hai ga-

ra-ri- yā, kutch kam- ti na mujh ko ho — — — gi, kutch

kam- ti na mujh ko ho — — — gi me-rā Yi-su Ma-sih hai ga-

ra- ri- ya — — — me-rā Yi-su Ma-sih hai ga- ra- ri- yā.

Chorus: Merā Yisu Masih hai garariyā,
(Jesus Christ is my Shepherd,)
Kutch kamti na mujh ko hogi.
(Nothing shall I lack.)

1. Mujhe hari hari ghās charātā
(He leads me in green pastures)
Aur nirmal pāni pilātā;
(And gives me water to drink;)
Mujhe bhukh pyās na hogi,
(I shall never hunger nor thirst,)
Merā Yisu Masih hai garariyā.
(Jesus Christ is my Shepherd.)

# Psalm 24.1-4 in Luganda

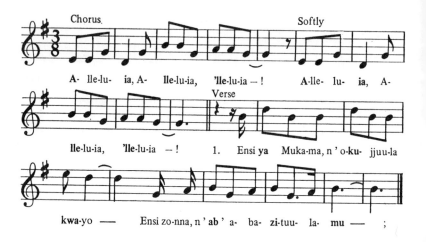

Chorus, Softly

A- lle-lu- ia, A- lle-lu-ia, 'lle-lu-ia — ! A-lle- lu- ia, A-

Verse

lle-lu-ia, 'lle-lu-ia — ! 1. Ensi ya Muka-ma, n ' o-ku- jjuu-la

kwa-yo — Ensi zo-nna, n ' ab ' a- ba- zi-tuu- la- mu — ;

Chorus: Alleluia, Alleluia, 'lleluia!
Alleluia, Alleluia. 'lleluia!

1. Ensi ya Mukama, n ' okujjuu-la kwayo,
   (The earth is the Lord's, and its fulness,)
   Ensi zonna, n ' ab ' ab'azituulamu;
   (The world and the people who dwell there;)

2. Kubanga yagisimba ku nnyanja,
   (It is he who has placed it on oceans,)
   Yaginyweza ku mazzi amangi.
   (Who has made the earth firm on the seas.)

3. An ' alirinnya ku lusozi lwa Mukama?
   (But who may ascend the Lord's mountain?)
   An ' aliyimirira mu kifo kye ' kitukuvu?
   (Who shall stand in his glorious place?)

4. Oy ' alin ' emikon ' emirung ', n ' omutim 'omulongoofu;
   (The man who has clean hands and pure heart,)
   Atayimusanga mmeeme y' eri bitaliimu.
   (Who refuses to worship the false.)

The Chorus is sung at the beginning, and at the end of each verse.

# THE PSALMS ARE FOR SINGING

## Tamil lyric from Psalm 121

Chorus

Kăn-gă- lai yē — rĕ-du- pĕn — — mā-mē-ru  nē-rāy, yĕn

‖: Semi-Chorus

kăn-gă- lai  yē — rĕ-du- pĕn.  Vin-  măn un-  -dā- ki- ya  vit-
Repeat Semi-Chorus :‖

tă- kă  ni-dă  mirunthu  yĕn- nil-la  vōt-  tā-sai  yĕn —
Back to beginning

dră. nu-kē  va-rum.  Kăn-gă- lai  yē —  rĕ-du-  pēn.

Chorus:        Kăngălai yērĕdupēn māmēru nērāy,
               (Mine eyes I will lift them straight above),
               Yĕn kăngălai yērĕdupēn.
               (Mine eyes I will lift them up.)

Semi-Chorus:   Vinman undākiya vittăkă nidă mirunthu
               (From creator of heaven and earth and worker of wonders)
               Yĕnnilla vōttāsai yĕndră nukē varum.
               (Countless help I will receive.)

1.             Kālai tăllădă vōttār,
               (He does not let my foot stumble,)
               Urangāthu kăppăvăr,
               (He who keeps does not sleep,)
               Kālai tăllădă vōttār.
               (He does not let my foot stumble.)
               Vēlaiyil nindrie rāvēlărai kăppăvăr
               (He who always keeps us)
               Kālaiyum mālaiyum kănnurăngārăvăr.
               (Day and night does not sleep.)

The verses are sung to the same tune as the Chorus and Semi-Chorus,
which are repeated after each verse.

123

## Psalm 136 Gelineau setting

2.     Who **alone** has wrought **marvellous works,** (Solo)
Great is his love, love without end, (All)
Whose **wisdom** it **was** made the **skies,** (Solo)
Great is his love, love without end, (All)
Who **spread** the **earth** on the **seas,** (Solo)
Great is his love, love without end. (All)

3.     It was **he** who **made** the great **lights,** (Solo)
Great is his love, love without end, (All)
The **sun** to **rule** in the **day,** (Solo)
Great is his love, love without end, (All)
The **moon** and **stars** in the **night,** (Solo)
Great is his love, love without end. (All)

4.     The firstborn of the Egyptians he **smote,** (Solo)
Great is his love, love without end, (All)
Brought Israel out from their **midst,** (Solo)
Great is his love, love without end, (All)
**Arm** outstretched, with **power** in his **hand,** (Solo)
Great is his love, love without end. (All)

During the present century a Frenchman, Joseph Gelineau, has composed special settings of Psalms for congregational singing, and a Christian group called the "Grail" have made his work widely known.

One of the psalms in which the writer drew special attention to the singing is Psalm 98. "O sing to the Lord a new song . . ." (v. 1). "Break forth into joyous song and sing praises. Sing praises to the Lord with the lyre (*kinnor*) and the sound of melody! With trumpets (long trumpets) and the sound of the horn (*shofar*) . . ." (vv. 4–6).

# Comment on Psalm 98: A Psalm to be sung

## THEME

What were the worshippers singing so joyfully about? They were singing because they recognized God as being in control of all the world. "He is Lord".

Their psalm is in three parts:

**Vv. 1–3:** God has been Lord (in the past).
**Vv. 4–6:** God is Lord (in the present).
**Vv. 7–9:** God will be Lord (in the future).

## USE

The Israelites probably sang this psalm at their autumn festival, the Festival of the Renewing of the Covenant, during which the worshippers "enthroned" God. See General Note A, p. 46, and note on p. 109.

## NOTES

**Ps. 98.1a: A new song.** Some people think that the Israelites first used Psalm 98 when they had returned from exile in Babylon. If this is so, we can see why they called it a "new" song. God had indeed shown His care for them in a new way.

But it is more likely that they meant that God had kept His promise and had given them a new year of harvest. Note the words "steadfast love" and "faithfulness" in v. 3a. See note on Psalm 96.1.

**Ps. 98.1b: He has done marvellous things.** In this verse the writer was remembering that God had shown that He was Lord in times past. In a similar way Christians recollect in their worship what God has done in times past. This is one reason why the Bible is read in Church. And it is an essential part of the Holy Communion service to worship "in remembrance of" the death of Jesus (1 Cor. 11.24).

The writer of Psalm 98 and the worshippers who used the psalm were able to say this because they recognized that it was God Himself who was active in the events of the past. We have already seen in our study of other psalms that this is how their writers looked at life. See notes on pp. 29, 46, and 97. They do not simply say "We have escaped from disaster". They said "God has rescued us". They needed "faith" to be able to say that, just as a patient in hospital today needs faith to say "God is healing me" rather than simply saying "I am getting better".

**Ps. 98.2b. He has revealed his vindication in the sight of the nations.** A better translation is "He has revealed his righteousness (or justice) to all the nations" (NEB).

When God gave new life to the Israelites' farms, or rescued their soldiers from their enemies, He was not only showing the Israelites themselves what He was like. By acting in this way, God was showing this to other nations also. The Israelites often forgot that God was concerned for other nations. See note on Psalm 96.3.

**Ps. 98.4: Make a joyful noise.** We have seen how the Israelites outwardly showed their joy concerning the goodness of God, e.g. by shouting and clapping and dancing and making music.

Two other psalms in which we see this clearly are 147 and 150. In Psalm 147 we read "It is good to sing praises to God" (v. 1) and "Make melody to our God upon the lyre (*kinnor*)" (v. 7). But in most of Psalm 147 worshippers are giving the reasons why they made music:

Vv. 1–6: Because God is in control of His creation and supports those with whom He has a Covenant.

Vv. 7–11: Because God makes the soil fertile.

Vv. 12–20: Because God has taken special care of Jerusalem.

Psalm 150 is another Hymn of Praise. It has the shout "Alleluia" at the beginning and at the end, and all of it concerns the praising of God:

Where? (v. 1)—"In His Temple, but not only in the Temple."

Why? (v. 2)—"Because of His great deeds."

How? (vv. 3–5)—"With dances and every musical instrument you have."

By whom? (v. 6)—"Every living thing."

**Ps. 98.9: He will judge.** This verse comes in the third part of the psalm, the part in which the worshippers are singing about the things that God will do in the future. They have the faith to believe that God will one day complete His victory over all that is evil.

Later the Israelites realized that the world would see God as King when the Messiah-King came. See Isaiah 9.7.

When Jesus came He said that this had now begun to happen. "The Kingdom of God is at hand" (Mark 1.15). But God's sovereignty was still not complete, so Jesus taught His disciples to pray "Thy Kingdom come" (Matt. 6.10).

St Paul said that in every Holy Communion service Christians pro-

"The leader sings the verses" (p. 119)—while the people wait to sing the chorus.

A "revivalist" singer in India does exactly this, at the microphone.

claim Christ's death "until He comes", i.e. that we worship in the faith that God will one day complete His work.

The Book of Revelation has a song of confidence about the future: "I heard every creature . . . saying, to Him who sits on the throne . . . be honour and glory and might for ever and ever" (Rev. 5.13).

In times of uncertainty we find it difficult to believe that God is in control of events. It is with words like these, "He will judge with righteousness", that our confidence is renewed. See also 96.9, 10.

## STUDY SUGGESTIONS

CONTENT

1. (a) What sort of musical instruments did the Israelites use as they worshipped, i.e. were they instruments which they blew? plucked? or beat? or shook?

   (b) What instruments did the Levites chiefly use in the Temple worship?

2. For what two main reasons did the Israelites sing the Psalms, rather than say them?

3. What is a "metrical psalm"?

BIBLE

4. What do the writers tell us about the way in which the worshippers sang the Psalms, in each of the following passages?

   (a) Ps. 33.2   (b) Ps. 67.4   (c) Ps. 27.6

5. (a) Are there songs which people are singing in your country today, in which one person sings the verses and everyone else sings a chorus? If so, give an example, and say what the chorus is.

   (b) In each of the following psalms it is possible to pick out the verse which was sung as a chorus. Say which it is, in each case: Psalms: 46, 49, 56, 62, 67, 80, 99, 107, 118.

6. Each of the following passages is about people making music. Say in each case what they were doing as they made music:

   (a) Gen. 31.27   (b) Num. 21.17   (c) Judg. 7.18, 20   (d) Judg. 11.34   (e) 1 Sam. 16.16–23   (f) 1 Chron. 15.25–28   (g) 2 Chron. 35.25   (h) Ps. 98.5

7. Psalms 147 and 150 are like Psalm 98 because through them the people shout their joy outwardly.

   What is the chief difference between the longer Psalm 147 and the shorter Psalm 150?

DISCUSSION AND RESEARCH

8. "Songs and psalms and hymns are a necessity, not a luxury, for worshippers" (p. 116). What is your opinion? Give your reasons.

9. (a) How important is singing to the people of your country? i.e.

what difference would it make to them if they were not able to sing?

(b) On what occasions do people mostly sing in your country?

(c) What sort of instruments have the people of your country traditionally used: (i) in worship? (ii) at other times?

10. In General Note B five different ways in which Christians sing the psalms have been described.

Which two of these ways are most suitable for the congregation you know best? Give reasons for your choice.

11. Which hymns from the Hymnbook of your Church are based on psalms?

12. "The Israelites outwardly showed their joy concerning the goodness of God" (p. 126).

(a) In what ways, if any, should Christians outwardly show their joy?

(b) What are the special reasons which Christians have for expressing joy in worship?

13. "Many Christians worship God by creating new psalms 'in the spirit of' the writers who created the 150 Psalms in the Bible" (p. 117).

(a) Write a new psalm of your own along these lines. (If you are studying in a group, work out a new psalm together.)

(b) Comment on the difference between the psalm you have written and the Psalms in the Old Testament.

# Shouts of Joy
## Psalm 100

### THEME

1. THE EXPERIENCE: BELONGING TO THE CONGREGATION

Twelve Christians of the Zande tribe in the Southern Sudan were standing under a mango tree. They had met in the bush to worship God because soldiers had burnt their church and had forbidden Christians to meet together except in a few large towns. As they had no books, members of the congregation reminded each other of the words of hymns and prayers and Bible passages, and took turns in leading the service. One of them left the service before the end, and set off on a long and very dangerous journey through the bush to try to obtain some hymnbooks from a town.

In a Theological College in Birmingham, England, a Communion service was in progress for students and staff. They had reached the part where they usually said the Confession together. On this occasion each took a piece of paper and wrote on it words of confession. Then he put it in an envelope, which he closed and passed to his neighbour. His neighbour tore it up, threw it into a basket, and after a silence the minister declared that God had forgiven them. Through this action staff and students experienced a one-ness with each other and thus a one-ness with God.

A congregation in one of the small churches of the Mangyan Church in Mindoro in the Philippines had just finished their evening service. The leader pushed bundles of bamboo into a fire, and when the bundles had taken light, gave one to each member as a torch. So the worshippers walked home across the mountain, bringing their lights with them into every home.

A woman came out of a church in Canada together with the three or four hundred other members. As she walked home, another worshipper asked her if she had enjoyed the service. She said, "I neither liked it nor disliked it. But I must have some roots somewhere to keep my marriage going. Joining in these services encourages me to go on being faithful to my husband. So I come every week."

Nearly every Christian who reads these accounts of worship will have had similar experiences. If we have, we will have found that in some way we needed to worship with other Christians and that they needed to worship with us. It was not enough to pray at home and alone.

The Israelites felt that they were losing something which was as necessary as food and drink if they could not join the congregation of worshippers. See note on Psalm 42.2. Those who first used Psalm 100 sang or shouted it out of this sort of experience, i.e. from the joy of belonging to the congregation.

We have already seen that Psalm 72 also came out of this experience of belonging to a group, i.e. to the nation of Israel. In the case of Psalm 72 the worshippers were thinking of the nation in all its activities. In Psalm 100 they were thinking mainly of the nation at its worship in the Temple.

As they rejoiced that they belonged to the congregation, they rejoiced at the same time that they belonged to God Himself. "We are the sheep of his pasture"; see note on Psalm 23.1. We now turn to what they said about God.

2. THE RECOGNITION OF GOD

The following four words and phrases point to the truth about God which they saw:

1. *The Lord is God* (v. 3a). I.e. the Lord whom we worship, He alone is God. He is the one true God. See note on Psalm 96.5.

2. *He made us* (v. 3b). By saying this they were not simply looking

back to a time when God began the creation of the world. They were thinking: "He came. He made us. We belong to Him. Because we belong to Him, we must give account to Him of the way we use His world and our own lives." See note on Psalm 100.3b.

3. *His steadfast love endures for ever* (v. 5b). See note on p. 37. The Israelites believed in God's steadfast love (Hebrew: *chesed*) because they remembered the great generosity which He had shown to them and the Covenant which He had made with them. See Psalm 136, in which the same sentence occurs in all twenty-six verses.

4. *His faithfulness* (v. 5c). According to Psalm 43.3 God is "true", i.e. He is reliable. See note on p. 52. In that verse the writer used the Hebrew word *emeth*. In Psalm 100 the Hebrew word which is translated "faithfulness" is *emunah*. These two Hebrew words have the same meaning, i.e. "God keeps His promises; He is steady, unchangeable, constant. You can rely on Him."

### 3. THE RESPONSE

We see the worshippers' response to God chiefly in what they did. This is shown in the following phrases:

*Make a joyful noise* (v. 1). Human beings do not always show their joy by making a noise, but they very often do, e.g. at a football match or at the birth of a child or at a New Year festival. See note on Psalm 100.1.

*Serve with gladness* (v. 2a). St Paul said "God loves a cheerful giver" (2 Cor. 9.7).

*Come* (v. 2b); *Enter* (v. 4a). It is true that all life is worship. "If we live, we live to the Lord" (Rom. 14.8). But there are times when it is necessary to withdraw from other activities in order to worship. When the Israelites first used this psalm, it was the whole nation who "came" and "entered" the Temple courtyards and worshipped God. But most Christians today, when they come to worship in a church, have to separate themselves from many of their friends and relatives.

*Give thanks* (v. 4c). One way in which Israelites expressed their thanks was by sacrifices. "Bring sacrifices and thank-offerings" (2 Chron. 29.31). When they gave thanks they were recognizing two facts. See note on Psalm 96.8.

*Bless his name* (v. 4c). I.e. praise God. See note on pp. 81 and 83.

The plan of Psalm 100 is in two parts, each of which has the same pattern:

**Vv. 1–3:** "Come and worship God" (vv. 1, 2) because we belong to Him (v. 3).

**Vv. 4, 5:** "Come and worship God" (v. 4) because His love endures for ever (v. 5).

There are many hymns of thanksgiving which have the same plan

"Make a joyful noise to the Lord!" (Ps. 100.1).

This Trinidadian is famous for the joyful noise he makes by his singing and guitar playing.

How joyful is our worship of God? What makes it joyful?

as Psalm 100, e.g. Psalm 147, which has three parts: vv. 1–6, vv. 7–11, and vv. 12–20. In each part we see:
First, a call: "Praise the Lord" (v. 1).
Secondly, the reason for praising: "For he is gracious" (v. 1b).

## USE

1. It is likely that the Israelites used Psalm 100 in the same way in which they used Psalm 96, i.e. at the Festival of the Enthronement of God. See General Note A, p. 46 and note on p. 109. Probably they shouted or sang it outside the entrance to the Temple, and afterwards passed through the gates into the courtyards around the Temple.

2. Later on, when the Jews worshipped in synagogues, they used this psalm every morning. Many Christians have also used it as part of a daily morning service.

3. When Christians use it today, verse 5 is often sung as a chorus.

## NOTES

**Ps. 100.1: Make a joyful noise.**

1. A man may make a noise because he is feeling "jolly" rather than "joyful". He is jolly (or "carefree") because things have turned out well for him. He has got a new job with better pay. Or he has recovered from an illness. Or his son has passed his exam. Or the rain which his garden needs has come at last. But if the new job is too difficult or his illness returns he may lose his jollity.

2. Joy is something different. A man is joyful if he has something precious which no one can take away. On the evening before Jesus was killed He showed that He had this sort of joy: "May my joy be in you" (John 15.11). "No one will take your joy from you" (John 16.22). When St Paul was in prison and did not expect to be set free, he could write, "I rejoice in the Lord greatly" (Phil. 4.10).

3. It is therefore right and good to rejoice even when suffering and sin seem to be increasing in the world. To rejoice is not to shut one's eyes to evil: it is to look through the evil to the Lord who is good (v. 5).

A visitor was going round the Christian leprosy settlement at Ongino in Uganda and meeting people of all sorts. After an hour he said, "But where are the patients?" Then they told him that all the people whom he had been meeting were the patients. He had not expected to find lepers who had joy.

4. When someone who believes in God is joyful he shows it in worship. Israelite worshippers, as they used Psalm 100, were shouting and singing and dancing and holding each others hands and clapping

and stamping. Christians have even more reason to show joy in their worship. But at church services they often show *less* joy!

**Ps. 100.1: All the lands.** Those who used Psalm 100, used it because they had experienced belonging to the worshipping congregation of Israelites. They knew that they were the People whom God had chosen, and with whom He had made a Covenant. "We are His people" (Ps. 100.3c).

But at the same time they knew that they were only a part of the whole creation to which God gave life. So in this psalm they remembered all created beings, "all the lands", and joined with them in praising God.

Christians also need to worship in these two ways:

1. They meet together, apart from other people. They meet in order to remember what God has done, to get support from God and from each other in order to serve Him in the world.

2. They worship in such a way that they become aware of those who are outside. They become aware of other Christians and of those who are not Christians. See notes on Psalms 67.2 and 96.3.

The "Ashram" or religious community at Jyotiniketan is in a part of North India where most people are Hindus. A visitor who was present at their 5 a.m. prayers noticed that the Christian members of the ashram prayed for Hindus and used some Hindu prayers, and that there were some Hindus worshipping with them.

In a church in Geneva in Switzerland, the whole wall which the congregation faces is made of glass. Outside this glass wall stands a tall cross, with houses and factories and streets around it. This has been done so that people worshipping inside the church may think about people outside it, and may also realize that God Himself is outside as well as inside.

Church services or prayer-meetings in a house are harmful if, as a result of them, the worshippers separate themselves from the life of those outside, e.g. if the worshippers fail to meet the needs of those "outside" or if they fail to work together with others "outside" whom God is using to do His work in the world. For this reason Christians need to limit the number of times when they meet together apart from the world.

So Christians need (1) to meet apart from others, and yet (2) to share fully in the life of those others. This is not easy. The leaders of the churches in an area where there was no theological college once received the following message: "There is now enough money to help you to build a college. If you accept this money, you will have to decide whether to build it in a quiet place in the country or in the city." Those leaders had to solve the same problem which any leader of worship has to solve.

**Ps. 100.3b: It is He that made us.** There are two Hebrew words which are used to refer to God as maker: *bara* (usually translated "create") and *asah* (usually translated "make"). In this verse the word is *asah*. Those who shouted for joy because God was their Maker were pointing to three truths:

1. *Dependence* upon God. Human beings depend upon God, who is the Maker and Owner of the world. He not only made the world in the beginning, but He continues to give it its life. "Thou renewest the face of the ground" (Ps. 104.30).

2. *Obedience* to God. Human beings live well in so far as they obey the will of God who made them. The maker of an article is the one who knows best how to use it. "Thy hands have made me . . . give me understanding that I may learn thy commandments" (Ps. 119.73).

3. The *purpose* of God. When God began the world He had a plan for its completion and its ending. Nothing can overcome the plan which He has made. That is the meaning of "Thus says the Lord . . . 'I am the first and I am the last'" (Isa. 44.6).

## STUDY SUGGESTIONS

WORDS

1. Psalm 100 starts with an invitation to people to worship God: "Make a joyful noise" (v. 1). There are six other words and phrases in this Psalm which are also invitations to worship.
   (a) What are these six?
   (b) In what way do these six differ from the similar words used in Psalm 96?

2. The Hebrew word *emunah* (Ps. 100.5c) refers to God, and is here translated "faithfulness".
   Which *four* of the following words have the same or nearly the same meaning as "faithfulness"?
   humility   loyalty   trustworthiness   importance   reliability
   steadiness   authority

3. (a) Which four of the following words have the same or nearly the same meaning as "jollity"?
   cheerfulness   refreshment   light-heartedness   merriment
   consolation   gaiety   comfort
   (b) What is the difference between the meaning of these four words and the meaning of "joy"?

CONTENT

4. On what occasions did the Israelites probably use Ps. 100?

5. Choose two of the truths about God which Ps. 100 contains, and say which verses contain each of these truths.

6. What *two* facts about themselves did Israelites bear in mind when they gave thanks to God in the words of Psalm 100?

7. (a) In what way are vv. 1 and 2 of Psalm 100 like v. 4?
   (b) In what way is v. 3 like v. 5?

BIBLE

8. (a) What phrase do we find in Psalms 100.5; 106.1; 107.1; 118.1; 136.1?
   (b) How would you explain the meaning of this phrase to a young child?

9. (a) To whom were the writers referring in the following passages: Pss. 33.8; 66.4; 96.1; 98.3b; 100.1?
   (b) What was the attitude of the writer of Psalm 100 towards such people?

10. "A man is joyful if he has something precious which no one can take away" (p. 133).
    Read the following passages about joy, and in each case,
    (i) Say if possible who was being joyful;
    (ii) Give the reason for the joy:
    (a) Luke 10.17 (b) Luke 19.37 (c) John 16.22 (d) John 16.24
    (e) Acts 5.41 (f) Acts 8.6–8 (g) Acts 13.48–51 (h) Acts 16.34
    (i) Gal. 5.22 (j) 1 Pet. 1.8

11. It is said on p. 135 that when writers in the Old Testament refer to God as "Creator" they also point to additional important truths about Him; e.g.
    (i) that they depend upon Him, or
    (ii) that they owe Him obedience, or
    (iii) that He has a purpose for what He has created.
    Which additional truth does the writer of each of the following passages point to as he calls God "Creator":
    (a) Ps. 100.3 (b) Ps. 104.10–13 (c) Isa. 45.9–13 (d) Isa. 66.22, 23 (e) Rom. 8.18–23

12. (a) In what way is Psalm 136 different from the other Psalms?
    (b) How can it best be used as part of Christian congregational worship.

DISCUSSION AND RESEARCH

13. Imagine that you are:
    (a) The man leaving the Zande congregation to obtain some hymnbooks (p. 120);
    (b) The Canadian woman who wanted to go on loving her husband (p. 130);
    Say in each case in what way you think that you could be helped by belonging to a congregation.

14. "Israelite worshippers were shouting and singing and dancing and holding each other's hands and clapping and stamping..." (p. 133).
(a) Do people often worship in this way in the Church to which you belong?
(b) If so, say why they do. If not, say why they do not.
(c) Describe an act of Christian worship at which you have been present and in which the worshippers showed their joy outwardly. Say in what ways they expressed their joy.
15. "All life is worship" (p. 131).
(a) What does this mean?
(b) What is your own opinion?
(c) Give two examples from everyday life to illustrate your opinion.
16. "Christians need (1) to meet apart from others; and yet (2) to take part in the life of those 'others'" (p. 134).
If this is true, then
(a) How often should Christians meet together?
(b) If you had been one of the Church leaders referred to on p. 134, would you have built the college in the country or in the city? Give your reasons.

# The Eagle
# Psalm 103

## THEME

### 1. THE EXPERIENCE: SAMENESS

When people find that things remain the same they may feel comfortable, or they may feel the opposite, and lose hope.

It is a comfort to eat the same sort of food that we ate yesterday, to see the same buildings as we go to work, to greet the same people in the same way we have greeted them before, to begin work at the same time, to do work well because it is familiar to us, to come home to the same home and to find the other members of the family there. When we have experiences of this kind, we are made steady and secure. In situations of this sort, it is not difficult to maintain law and order.

For the Israelites it was a great comfort to know that God remained the "same". Like a good parent He was "consistent", i.e. His care for His people never changed. See the note on God's "truth" on p. 52.

On the other hand there are things which may lead us to despair just because they remain the same.

There is sameness in human suffering and sin. The newspapers report the same sort of wars and crimes. Today there are more than ten million refugees in the world. Year after year there are floods in Bangladesh. Jews are being persecuted in many countries simply because they are Jews. In every continent some people are still oppressed and persecuted simply because of the colour of their skin.

Personal troubles, too, may seem to remain the same. One man, as soon as he has found a job, loses it because he always comes late to work. Another has the same pain in his lungs at the same time every year. A mother may make the same mistakes in bringing up each child she bears. Millions of people know that their sins and failures remain the same year after year.

When people meet this kind of evil and suffering being repeated over and over again, they may behave in various ways.

(a) They may become "fatalistic", i.e. they may think that "fate" or "chance" controls all events.

(b) Or they may become as "pessimistic" as the writer of Ecclesiastes was, who wrote "What has been is what will be, and what has been done is what will be done . . . What is crooked cannot be made straight" (Eccles. 1.9, 15).

(c) Or they may become "cynical", i.e. speak as though evil controls all actions.

The Israelites who used this psalm had certainly experienced the sameness of evil and suffering. They had themselves repeatedly been unfaithful to God. They had experienced one war after another. And they had such things as these in mind as they sang this psalm. Remembering such things, what did they feel? How did they behave?

## 2. THE RECOGNITION OF GOD

1. The people who used this psalm saw beyond the sameness of evil and suffering. In spite of it they recognized God as One who gives new life, "your youth is renewed like the eagle's" (v. 5). According to the folklore of many countries eagles do not die, but start life again by flying into the sun, and the sun gives them new life-giving heat. So the Israelites recognized God as offering a new start to people who had forgotten that change was possible. They expressed the same thing in the great words in vv. 3–5: "forgives", "heals", "redeems", "steadfast love". In the Bible as a whole writers repeat this truth continually, e.g. "Behold, I am doing a new thing" (Isa. 43.19); "If any one is in Christ, he is a new creation" (2 Cor. 5.17). See notes on Psalms 96.1 and 98.1a.

2. We read here of two groups of people to whom God always offers a new start, people who seem to be "stuck" in the same situations for ever.

(a) First there are the *wrong-doers*: "He forgives all your iniquity" (3a); "He crowns you with steadfast love" (4b). "Steadfast love" is used to translate the Hebrew word *chesed* which means that God gives more than His people deserve. See note on Psalm 23. This love "abounds" (v. 8), i.e. it overflows, as when a generous shopkeeper gives a customer more than he or she has paid for.

It is the unexpectedness of God's forgiveness which is emphasized in this psalm. Those who are forgiven are continually surprised. When Jesus taught that God forgave in this way, many of His hearers thought that such teaching would make people lazy and immoral: "He is leading the people astray" (John 7.12), i.e. "if people think that God forgives so completely, they will not try to be good any longer".

We have seen the meaning of God's forgiveness in our study of Psalm 51. See also note on Psalm 130.8b. Here we may notice two other ways of describing it in picture-language:

(i) To God, the past and the sins which we committed in the past are as far away as the east is from the west (v.12). These words have a new meaning for us who saw the division which existed for forty years between the eastern European group of nations, e.g. Russia, and those who were joined with the western group, e.g. Britain and the U.S.A.

(ii) God, like a good parent, has not let the mistakes of the past affect the way He treats His children in the present: "the Lord has compassion" (v. 13).

(b) Secondly, God gives new life to *sufferers*: "He heals all your diseases" (v. 3). God cares about the things which our bodies and minds need. (Nowhere in the Bible do we read that God regards our "souls" as important while regarding our bodies and minds as not important.)

(c) We notice, more briefly, other words in this psalm which show what the worshippers recognized about God:

*Holy* (v. 1). By this the worshippers were saying that God is different from human beings, and has a far greater hatred of the evil which spoils people's lives. See note on p. 29.

*Just* (v. 6). They were saying that God protects people who are too weak to protect themselves. See note 4, "He judges", on p. 107.

*Reveals* himself (v. 7). God has not remained hidden and apart from human beings. He has "made His ways known", as He did to Moses (Exod. 33.13).

*Knows* and *Remembers* (v. 14). See the notes on Psalm 139.1 and Psalm 8.4.

### 3. THE RESPONSE

1. The worshippers responded *whole-heartedly*. "All that is within me, bless!" (v. 1). Because God is generous beyond all expectation human beings can open the whole of themselves towards Him, and

139

they do so in worship. We remember the Holy Communion prayer, "Unto whom all hearts are open, all desires known, and from whom no secrets are hidden". So people can bring themselves to God with all their thinking and all their feeling (their joy, disappointment, anger, doubt). They do not need to leave anything outside (as they leave a wet umbrella in the porch outside the church).

2. The worshippers *accepted* what God offered, e.g. the unexpected gift of forgiveness.

3. The worshippers responded by adoring God in the company of others. Verses 19–22 contain a picture of the whole creation adoring Him. In this picture it is as if God were a king or a great chief and His important subjects were shouting, "Long live the king!" All living creatures are represented by His messengers (called "angels" in v. 20) and politicians ("mighty ones" in v. 20) and soldiers ("hosts" in v. 21) and attendants ("ministers" in v. 21).

The plan of this response is as follows:

**Vv. 1–5:** As individuals, we know God's love.

**Vv. 6–18:** As a nation, we know it. (This section is in three strophes: vv. 6–10, 11–14 and 15–18.)

**Vv. 19–22a:** In response to His love, we join in adoring Him.

**Vv. 22b:** A chorus.


## USE

In the congregational worship of some Churches, the first five verses only of this psalm are sung (or vv. 1–5 with vv. 19–22), as part of the Communion service.

When a chorus is to be sung, verse 1 (or vv. 1 and 2) makes the best chorus.

The hymn "Praise, my soul" is an interpretation of this psalm. Here is the first verse, which is based on vv. 1–5:

> Praise, my soul, the King of Heaven,
> To His feet thy tribute bring;
> Ransomed, healed, restored, forgiven,
> Who like thee his praise should sing?
> Praise Him! Praise Him!
> Praise the everlasting King.

Many families use vv. 1 and 2 as a "grace" at meal-times, and many individuals use them as an "arrow prayer" at any time of day or night. David Livingstone used them in this way when he was becoming weak from fever during his travels in central Africa. The American explorer, Stanley, had promised to send him men and medicine, but six months had passed and the men did not come. Then one day they came and he

"God offers a new start to people who have forgotten that change was possible" (p. 138).

This man in Hong Kong had his hand cut off in an accident. To his and everyone's astonishment, doctors were able to attach the hand to the arm. Today he can again use chop-sticks.

wrote in his diary, "I do most devoutly thank the Lord for his goodness in bringing my men . . . three came today and how thankful I am I cannot express . . . Bless the Lord, O my soul, and all that is within me, bless His holy Name. Amen."

## NOTES

**Ps. 103.1: Bless the Lord.** There are very many psalms in which God is "blessed" or praised. But here we may note two kinds of praise-psalms:

First, those in which God is praised because He has created and controls all *things*, e.g. Psalms 8; 19.1–6; 29; 104. Secondly, those in which He is praised because He has saved and taken care of His *people*. This psalm (103) is one of the second kind. See also Psalms 105, 111, 114, etc.

There are other psalms in which God is praised both for His creation of things and for His continued caring for His People, e.g. 33, 65, 136, 145.

**Ps. 103.3a: He forgives all your iniquity.** Why do people find it so difficult (or even impossible) to accept God's forgiveness? It must be for reasons such as these:

(a) They mistakenly think that God holds back His forgiveness, waiting for people to repent. But God forgives us even before we repent, and it is this act of His which calls out our repentance. See note on Psalm 51, p. 62.

(b) They know that if they accept it, they will be able to live better lives. And if their lives are better, God will call on them to *keep* them better. It seems to them that it is easier to stay unforgiven.

(c) They mistakenly think that continual sorrow for sin is the greatest Christian virtue. In fact the most important thing is to know how to start again after receiving forgiveness.

(d) They refuse to forgive someone else. A father refused to write letters to his son who was abroad because, he said, "he has wasted my money and does not deserve to hear from me". So long as that father holds back his forgiveness until his son has "deserved" it, of course he cannot understand that God forgives us although we do not deserve it (and perhaps he makes it difficult for his son also to understand this truth).

**Ps. 103.3b: He heals all your diseases.** But *how* does God heal? How can the man who gets the same sort of cough every time the wind is cold and wet experience His healing? Many Christians would answer along the following lines:

(a) God has made human beings one family, so that the members can help and heal each other. This is God's first way of healing. For example an employer is responsible for paying his workmen enough for them to be able to eat properly; otherwise they will be too weak to resist disease.

(b) God has given intelligence to human beings to discover the causes of disease and the ways in which people can be restored to health. And He calls men and women to train as doctors and nurses and to work to bring healing to other members of the human family. Through such workers God brings health to people who had never expected it, for example people suffering from leprosy who, until they took modern medicines, had thought they could never be healed. He saves people who suffer from pneumonia, by the use of penicillin.

(c) God offers to help people to find a new outlook in difficult circumstances. This is different from saying that God removes people from their unpleasant circumstances. For God does not do that; He does not prevent anyone from getting older, nor place anyone in a better climate.

People find a new outlook from knowing that God Himself is in control and that He loves us. An old man described his experience of this: "My wife died and at first I suffered terribly from loneliness. Then someone helped me to see that because I was lame and was usually at home, God could use me to listen to people. Grown-ups and children now come to me and tell me about their successes and their failures. It has been as happy as any time of my life, and a great surprise."

A Church Army worker in training got leprosy, and was told the disease was too far advanced to heal. Life became very hard indeed for him, and he was tempted to give up being a Christian. But someone said to him, "God has not given you up". He found he was still able to do hard work, and eventually he received his commission as a Church Army Captain.

**Ps. 103.13: As a father.** There are people who do not believe that there is any God, and who say they do not need any God. Their opinion is that religious people have felt so strongly the need for a Great Parent who never dies that they have invented one, and have called him "God".

It is just as reasonable to hold the opposite opinion: namely that since God does exist He shows His nature most clearly in a human parent. Jesus taught this. "If you want a picture of God in your minds when you pray", He said, "Use the word 'Father'" (see Matt. 6.9); "Look at human parents, even ordinary ones who make many mistakes, and you will get some idea of how God treats people" (see Matt. 7.11). He even called God "Abba" (which is like the English words "Daddy" or "Papa"). See Mark 14.36. But the word "Father" is only a picture-word. God is neither masculine nor feminine. See note on Psalm 96.10.

**Ps. 103.16: It is gone and its place knows it no more.** It is clear from vv. 15 and 16 that the people who used this psalm did not believe that a man could have fellowship with God after his death. This is true of other writers in the Old Testament, e.g. "In death there is no remembrance of thee" (Ps. 6.5).

See also Psalm 90, which many Christians know because of the version of it "O God our help in ages past". Its plan is:

Vv. 1, 2: Lord, you are eternal, and have sheltered mankind in the past.

Vv. 3–6: But our human lives are short.

Vv. 7–12: We deserve to be punished for our sins, but does punishment have to continue all our lives?

Vv. 13–17: Have pity on us, Lord!

Throughout this psalm the writer is saying "Since there is no life after death, do not let this life be all pain".

It is possible that there were some who held a different view. See Psalm 73.24: "Afterwards thou wilt receive me in glory"; Psalm 139.8: "If I make my bed in Sheol (the grave), thou art there!" But it is not certain that these writers believed they would have any continuing relationship with God after death.

However, in the Psalms we do see the foundations of a belief in life after death, e.g. in the words "steadfast love". Afterwards, through the teaching of Jesus, Christians saw that even death cannot separate us from such strong love. "I am sure that neither death nor life . . . nor anything in all creation will be able to separate us from the love of God in Christ Jesus our Lord." (Rom. 8.38, 39.)

**Ps. 103.18: Keep his covenant.** As we have seen, the Israelites thought of themselves as joined to God by a special agreement or "Covenant" (the Hebrew word used here is *berith* and there is no word in English which translates it better than "Covenant").

They regarded the events of which we read in Exodus 19.1–6 and 24.3–8 as the time when this Covenant was first established. See note on p. 46. There were two sides to this agreement. God on His side chose the Israelites as His people and promised to treat them with "steadfast love". The Israelites on their side knew that they could depend on God. They promised to be faithful to Him, and to live according to the laws which He had laid down for their happiness. In vv. 17 and 18 of this Psalm we see these two sides, "the steadfast love of the Lord is . . . to those who keep His covenant". It does not mean that God only loved the Israelites when they obeyed Him. It means that when they failed to obey Him, they were preventing themselves from receiving all the good things He was offering them.

Everything that the Israelites did, they did as part of this agreement, because by it they belonged to God. When they spoke of God's *chesed* ("steadfast love") they knew that God gave them His "*chesed*" because of the Covenant. See note on p. 37. When they sang a psalm, they sang it because they were joined to Him by the Covenant. As we have seen, they probably used many of the psalms in a New Year Festival of the Renewing of the Covenant.

We can see this in Psalm 95. Although the word "covenant" is not used, worshippers had the Covenant in mind. See v. 6 where "our maker" means not only "maker and preserver of the world" but also "maker and preserver of the covenant between us and God." See also v. 7 in which they call God "Shepherd" chiefly because He made a Covenant with them.

The plan of Psalm 95 is:

Vv. 1–7b: The leader calls to the worshippers to shout in praise of God (let us make a joyful noise), and gives reasons for praising Him.

Vv. 7c–11: He warns worshippers to obey God in their daily lives, unlike their ancestors with whom God made the Covenenat.

But the Israelites, as we know, often failed to keep their part of it.

It was the prophet Jeremiah who saw that a new Covenant was needed, through which God would "put His law in people's hearts" (Jer. 31.33). God did make a New Covenant, as Jesus said during the Last Supper: it was made by His dying (Mark 14.24). This is the Covenant by which Christians are joined to God, and which is renewed, for instance, at every Holy Communion service.

**Ps. 103.18: Remember to do.** We have seen the special meaning of the word "remembering" when it is used to describe God's activity. See note on Psalm 8.4.

In this verse it is clear that it is human beings who must remember. In the Bible the word "remembering" is not only used to mean thinking about past events: it is used to mean thinking about the past *so that it makes a difference to the present*. For example, v. 18b shows that "remembering" leads to obedience in the present. Remembering Jesus' death (as we do in the Holy Communion) is this kind of remembering.

## STUDY SUGGESTIONS

WORDS

1. "There are things which may lead us to despair just because they remain the same" (p. 137).
   Which *three* of the following words have the same or nearly the same meaning as that kind of "sameness":
   heaviness  monotony  repetition  smoothness  routine

CONTENT

2. In what way are the following three attitudes to life like each other: "fatalism"  "pessimism"  "cynicism"?
3. What thoughts did the writer of Psalm 103 have in mind when he used each of the following examples of picture language:

(a) the eagle (v. 5)
(b) the east and the west (v. 12)
(c) a father (v. 13)

## BIBLE

4. What truth contained in Psalm 103 is also contained in the following passages:
   Lam. 3.23   Ezek. 36.26   Ezek. 37.11–14   Rev. 21.1
5. In what way are Psalms 29 and 111 alike?
6. What do we learn about the Covenant between God and man in each of the following passages:
   (a) Ps. 89.34   (b) Jer. 31.33   (c) 1 Cor. 11.25?

## DISCUSSION AND RESEARCH

7. "Look at human parents . . . and you will get some idea of the way God treats people" (p. 143).
   (a) How far do you think children's feelings about their parents affect their feelings about God?
   (b) What are the advantages and disadvantages of calling God "Father"?
8. What would you reply to someone who said: "If people think that God forgives us before we repent, they will not try to be good any longer."
9. We read on p. 143 of the experience of a man whom God did not take out of his circumstances but to whom He gave a new attitude.
   Give another example of this sort of experience.
10. Four reasons are suggested on p. 142 why people fail to accept God's forgiveness. Give another reason.
11. In vv. 19–22 the Israelite worshippers compared God to a king on a throne with attendants round Him. As more and more countries cease to have kings and become republics:
    (a) Should Christians any longer compare God to a king or "chief"? Give your reasons.
    (b) Think of another word or phrase instead of "king" which we might use when speaking of the supreme authority of God; and say what the advantages and disadvantages of using it might be.
12. "It is not likely that these writers believed they would have any continuing relationship with God after death" (p. 144).
    What do you yourself believe about life after death? Give at least one reason for your answer.

# The Broken Chains
## Psalm 116

## THEME

### 1. THE EXPERIENCE: RECOVERY FROM DISTRESS

Nearly all human beings from time to time experience the joy of recovering from misery and distress.

Terrorists kidnapped a politician in South America and held him to ransom. Six months later they released him and he had the joy of meeting his wife again.

Doctors in Fiji operated on a boy's leg ten times in one year. Each time the leg gave the boy great pain. But after two years it healed completely, and he had the great pleasure of playing football again.

A law student from Cyprus who had failed to pass his "final" examination six times was successful the seventh time, and was able to begin work as a lawyer.

A West African woman who had been childless for fifteen years after her marriage at last gave birth to a son.

An official of an American bank who was travelling round the world felt ill during his journey, and was told by a doctor that he probably had cancer of the stomach. For the rest of the journey he lived in fear that he would soon die. When he returned to New York, an X-ray showed that it was not cancer which had caused his pain.

A boy arrived for the first time at a big school in Tanzania and discovered that he was the only boy from his tribe in the school. He felt extremely lonely, but a year later found that he had plenty of friends among the boys.

What do these people think and do in their joy? Often they do not *think* very much at all. They run off like nine of the lepers whom Jesus cured (Luke 17.17) and just celebrate their happiness with their friends. Or they simply believe that they have "been lucky".

Those who first used Psalm 116 had had an experience of "recovery". They had recovered from some great distress. Perhaps it was a serious illness ("the snares of death encompassed me" v. 3a), or national defeat in battle ("distress and anguish" v. 3b, "I was brought low" v. 6). Whatever the suffering was, the sufferers felt like prisoners who had been chained to the wall of their prison. The chains had now been broken, and they were free! They had peace. They could rest (see v. 7). As they rejoiced in their freedom, they saw that it was God Himself who had "broken the chains".

147

## 2. THE RECOGNITION OF GOD

Several times in this psalm the worshippers emphasized that it was *God* who had freed them, "He has heard" (v. 1), "He inclined his ear" (v. 2). See also vv. 6, 7, 8, 16.

They used three different words in v. 5 to describe the character of God who had done this for them. They said that He was "gracious" and "righteous" and "merciful".

Why did they interpret their recovery in this way? Why did they not say, "We have been lucky"? It was because they believed that they belonged to God (they were "His people"). They were accustomed to tell God about their troubles as part of their public worship. When joy came again they looked on God as the One who had rescued them, and so they told Him of their gratitude.

We see then that the worshippers were saying two things in particular.

1. They were saying, "God did this (i.e. it did not happen by chance or good luck)." The Israelites did not believe that anything took place by chance. (They had no word in their language for "fate", such as the Muslim's word "kismet".) What do we who read this today believe about "chance"? If we think that some things happen by chance, how do we distinguish between those events and the events which God causes? See note on pp. 151 and 152.

2. They were saying "God did it because we asked Him to do it (i.e. He 'heard' our prayer and did what we wanted)".

Pastor Joseph Nathaniel works among the many hill tribes who live in the jungly forests near Mysore in S. India. For many years he prayed that he and his fellow-workers should be allowed to enter a group of villages in one of the tribal areas. At last a headman gave permission for them to come into his village, and a hundred villagers met Christians for the first time. It was natural that Pastor Nathaniel should thank God for having "answered his prayers".

Certainly, if anyone has had this experience, even once, he is likely to be greatly strengthened in his belief in God. For instance, a man in Port Moresby who had many friends was desperately ill. His friends prayed for him all night, and in the morning he recovered, to the surprise of the doctors. The friends said, "God has answered our prayers." But God does not always answer prayers in this way. See notes on Psalm, 43.1 and 116.1a.

## 3. THE RESPONSE: THIS PSALM OF THANKSGIVING

We have seen that after having recovered from trouble, the worshippers recognized that it was God who had given them this recovery. So they "rendered" (v. 12) or "paid back" to God this psalm of gratitude.

As they used this psalm they were giving thanks in several ways:

"Thou hast delivered my soul from death" (Ps. 116.8).

While a group of Frenchmen were travelling across the Sahara Desert, their bus broke down, and they had only enough food and water for a few days. They waited for a rescue lorry to reach them. When it came, this man, Gilbert Dernaz, was still alive and was saved.

(a) They were acknowledging publicly what God had done. This is the real meaning of the word which is translated "call upon" in vv. 13 and 17.

(b) They were rededicating themselves to serve God faithfully, e.g. by making vows (vv. 14 and 18), by being God's servants (v. 16), and by symbolic actions. These actions were: to pour out part of the wine or water in a cup ("lift the cup" v. 13), and to sacrifice an animal (see v. 17).

(c) They were expressing their praise and thanksgiving, "Praise the Lord" (v. 19b).

Thus they showed their gratitude in outward and visible ways, as most people do who are really grateful to God. We read on p. 147 of a West African woman who was childless for fifteen years and then had a baby boy. At the next Harvest Festival she danced up the Church when the "thank-offerings" were being taken up, and the congregation clapped their hands to keep time with her dance. Then from her handkerchief she took six eggs and put them amongst the other offerings. Then she danced back to her seat.

A carpenter came to a Canadian minister and said, "I have been unfaithful to my wife. I know this is wrong and I can't forget it. But what can I do?". The minister said, "You kneel down and tell God what you've just told me. God has already forgiven you, so take courage." The man knelt down in the room. Then he stood up and they prayed together. From that time the man's life was different. And one day he presented to the church a sort of picture of the Last Supper. He had made it out of thirteen five-inch nails and a wooden board. He said, "I had to show God somehow that I was grateful."

On the fourth Thursday in November each year North Americans celebrate Thanksgiving Day. The first time that this took place was in Plymouth, USA, in November 1621. Previous pilgrims from Europe had died of starvation, but at last some pilgrims managed to grow enough food to live on, with the help of the local tribe of Indians, and so they held a special thanksgiving to God. Today some Americans still use the day as a time of thanksgiving to God, while for others it is only a holiday.

The plan of Psalm 116 is:

**Vv. 1–11:** The worshippers describe the distress from which God has now saved them.

**Vv. 12–19:** They express their gratitude to God, and rededicate themselves to serve Him.

## USE

1. When the Israelites used Psalm 116 during worship in the Temple, a leader probably sang or spoke it on behalf of the whole congregation.

This seems likely from the words, "*our* God" (v. 5), " in the presence of all his people" (vv. 14 and 18), and "in the courts of the house of the Lord" (v. 19).

It was one of the six Psalms of Praise of "Hallel" Psalms (113–18) which the Israelites sang on the great Festivals of Passover, Pentecost, and Tabernacles, as well as at other times.

2. Christians often sing Psalm 116 at Easter, perhaps because of verses 8 and 9, "Thou hast delivered my soul from death . . . I will walk before the Lord in the land of the living."

In some Churches the first part of the psalm is used as a prayer of thanksgiving by women after childbirth. The second part is often used as a prayer of preparation for the Holy Communion.

It is a good prayer for all who have special reason to thank God. A girl of eighteen opened her heart to God for the first time in her life and told Him honestly about all her life, the bad part as well as the good. At once she knew that she had received His forgiveness. She was so happy that she *ran* into a church and used this psalm (as well as her own words) as a thanksgiving.

A German pastor was imprisoned in 1936 because he opposed Hitler for the way he treated the Jews. For a long time he was overcome by his fear of death. Then the fear left him and he was able to think about death with confidence in God. He was so grateful for this change in himself that he repeated over and over again verses 12 and 13 of this psalm which he had memorized as a child: "What shall I render to the Lord for all his bounty to me? I will lift up the cup of salvation and call upon the name of the Lord."

A student making notes on this psalm wrote, "I hope that when the time comes for me to die I shall be able to use verse 7 as my prayer. "Return, O my soul, to your rest: for the Lord has dealt bountifully with you'."

## NOTES

**Ps. 116.1a: He has heard.** The writer clearly meant that God had "answered" his prayer. We may here consider two questions which people often ask on this subject.

1. When we are in trouble, and we pray, and later recover, is our recovery God's answer to our prayer? We cannot always say this. Millions of people recover from trouble, who never pray at all. Does recovery from trouble sometimes happen by chance?

Not all Christians are agreed on the answer to this question.

(a) Some point to Jesus' words in Matthew 10.29, "Not one sparrow will fall to the ground without your Father's will". They say that nothing happens by chance.

(b) Others believe that when God made the world, He allowed there to be chance in it. If this is true, then there are times when we can say "This happened by chance," and other times when we say "This is the answer of God." The following story illustrates this. A man living in Singapore made a will by which, if he died after 1 January five years later, his son would inherit $70,000. If he died before that date his business partners would receive the money. The son was poor and greatly needed the money. In fact the father was killed in a car accident on 3 January five years later.

2. "Does God always answer our prayers?"

Some people say, "Yes, He does. His answer may be 'Yes', or it may be 'No', or it may be 'Wait'. But He always answers." Another way of saying the same thing is as follows:

(a) God knows better than we do what we really need. If we have asked for something that would be harmful for us, then His answer will not be the answer we wanted.

(b) God considers the needs of all His people, not our own needs alone. This is another reason why God's answer is sometimes "No".

(c) God has not promised to take us out of all troubles. He has promised to give us the will and the spirit to face those troubles. St Paul asked God three times to take away his malaria or epilepsy (or whatever his "thorn" was). God's answer was to give him "sufficient grace" to endure it (see 2 Cor. 12.7–10). See notes on p. 98 and on Psalm 23.4a.

**Ps. 116.1b: My supplication.** In this psalm, as in very many other psalms, we see that the worshippers asked God for help. Jesus made it clear that His followers should "ask" (Matt. 7.7). St Paul wrote, "In everything by prayer and supplication with thanksgiving let your requests be made known to God" (Phil. 4.6). But what sort of requests should a Christian offer to God? See note on Ps. 43.1.

**Ps. 116.6: The Lord preserves the simple.** The Hebrew word which is translated "simple" means "believer", i.e. someone who has kept his faith in God through all the difficulties of living in a time of great change. It does not mean "uneducated" or "foolish" or "lacking in intelligence".

**Ps. 116.9: I walk before the Lord.**

1. NEB has "I will walk before the Lord . . .", which is probably a better translation. (It is not possible when reading Hebrew to know the exact tense of the verb.) If NEB is correct, then this was a promise which the grateful worshippers made to God.

2. The Hebrew verb *halach*, which is here translated "walk", does not mean to go forward on one's feet. It means to keep the will of God which He has shown to His people. The noun *halachah* means "the way" in which God wants His people to live. See Deuteronomy 5.33: "You shall walk in all the way which the Lord your God has com-

manded you." Christians also use the word "way" like this. See Acts 9.2: "If he found any belonging to the Way . . .". See also notes on Psalm 19 and Psalm 139.24.

**Ps. 116.15: Precious in the sight of the Lord is the death of his saints.**

1. Clearly this does not mean that God likes people to suffer and to die. It means that when a believer dies, God notices it and is concerned about it. "Even the hairs of your head are all numbered" (Luke 12.7).

2. The word "saints" translates the Hebrew word *chasid* (a word which is connected with *chesed*. See note on p. 37). The *chasid* people are not the very good people who keep all God's laws. From other psalms we see what they are:

(a) They are people who show *chesed*. They show the same sort of generosity that God shows to the people who are joined to Him by Covenant. "With the loyal (*chasid*) thou dost show thyself loyal" (Ps. 18.25a).

(b) They trust in the *chesed* of God rather than in the power of their own possessions. "The righteous (*chasid*) shall laugh at him saying, 'See the man who . . . trusted in the abundance of his riches'." (Ps. 52.6, 7.)

(c) They join in the worship of the Temple. "Sing praises to the Lord, O you his saints" (Ps. 30.4).

**Ps. 116.17: The sacrifice of thanksgiving.**

1. What is thanksgiving?

A person who is thankful to God is someone who knows that he depends upon God for all his existence and for all the things that help him to grow and develop. People who say that they believe that God exists but cannot thank Him are often independent people, i.e. people who find it hard to depend upon anyone, people who do not accept help from their friends, fearing that those friends in giving help would dominate them.

2. There are many other psalms in which we read words of thanksgiving.

Psalm 32 was St Augustine's favourite psalm. Like Psalm 116, it is mainly thanksgiving for God's forgiveness:

Vv. 1, 2: A person is happy when God has forgiven him.

Vv. 3–5: I suffered until I admitted my sinfulness, in body as well as in spirit.

Vv. 6–11: Let others learn from my experience.

Similarly Psalm 34 is mainly a thanksgiving, especially its first part (vv. 1–10). But throughout this psalm and especially in its second part (vv. 11–22) the writer is also giving instruction. He is teaching his pupils that only those who obey God will be really happy.

Other psalms which are mainly prayers of thanksgiving are: 18, 30, 65, 92, 107, 118, 124, 136, 138.

There are also many separate expressions of thanksgiving which come in psalms of another sort. Psalm 13 is a prayer to God from someone in great trouble, but it contains the words "My heart shall rejoice in thy salvation; I will sing to the Lord because He has dealt bountifully with me" (vv. 5 and 6).

But in every psalm the worshippers show in some way that they depend upon God. As we have seen, this is the attitude which makes it possible to thank God.

## STUDY SUGGESTIONS

### WORDS

1. Give four words which the writer of Psalm 116 used to show what God had done for him, e.g. "saved" (v. 6b).
2. The Hebrew word *chasid* is translated "saint" in Psalm 116.15. It is also used in the following Psalms:
   (a) 18.25a  (b) 30.4  (c) 50.5  (d) 52.9  (e) 86.2a  (f) 145.10 (g) 149.1
     (i) How is it translated in each of these passages in the RSV?
     (ii) How is it translated in these passages in any other Bible version you know?
     (iii) What is the difference between the way in which the writer of Psalm 116 used the word, and the way in which you use the word "saint" in ordinary conversation?
3. What is the meaning of each of the following words or phrases used in Psalm 116:
   (a) The simple (v. 6)  (b) Render (v. 12)  (c) The courts of the house of the Lord (v. 19).

### CONTENT

4. What made it possible for the writer of Ps. 116 to recognize that it was God who had saved him?
5. What two outward and visible actions did the worshippers perform, according to Psalm 116, to express their thanksgiving?
6. What words and phrases in Psalm 116 suggest that the whole congregation used it (probably led by one person)?

### BIBLE

7. The following psalms contain thanksgiving to God. Pick out one verse in each psalm which could be used as an arrow prayer of thanksgiving offered to God by anyone at any time:
   (a) 18  (b) 30  (c) 34  (d) 92  (e) 124  (f) 138
8. Read Psalm 32. For what do you think that the writer was thanking God?

9. Read the following passages and say in each case what the writer meant by the word "walk":
   (a) Exod. 16.4  (b) Lev. 26.3  (c) 2 Kings 10.31  (d) Micah 4.5a  (e) Micah 4.5b
10. Is it true to say that in Phil. 4.6 Paul summed up the thoughts of the writer of Psalm 116? Give reasons for your answer.

DISCUSSION AND RESEARCH

11. This chapter is headed "Broken Chains".
    (a) Why do you think this title was chosen?
    (b) Suggest another title for the chapter and give reasons for your choice.
12. Which verse or part of a verse in Psalm 116 would you choose to use as a chorus verse. Give a reason for your choice.
13. (a) Give one example from everyday life to show the truth of each of the following statements (from p. 152).
    (i) If we have asked for something that would be harmful to us, then God's answer will not be the answer we wanted.
    (ii) God considers the needs of all His people, not our own needs only. This is another reason why God's answer is sometimes "No".
    (b) What would you reply to someone who said: "It is a waste of time to ask God for anything. He will give it to you in any case if it is good for you"?
14. The worshippers were saying, "God did it", i.e. "it did not happen by chance" (p. 148).
    (a) What have the people of your country and language traditionally believed about "luck" or "chance"?
    (b) What words if any have they used for "luck"?
    (c) Is it possible for someone who believes that God is good and powerful to believe also that some things happen by chance? Give reasons for your answer.
15. A father and mother had a child who was paralysed. After many years she was cured and was able to walk and run. Her parents were so grateful to God that every Sunday for several years one of them visited the patients in a hospital near their home and took them little presents.
    (a) In what way is the behaviour of these parents like the behaviour of those who first used Psalm 116?
    (b) In what way is it different?
    (c) Give an example from your experience of other people behaving like these parents.
16. Write a short imaginary conversation between yourself and a friend beginning with the following remarks:

*Yourself*: During my illness I prayed for health and God heard my prayer.

*Friend*: I'm glad you're well again. But what makes you think that it was God who healed you?

# The Night-Watchman
## Psalm 130

### THEME

#### 1. THE EXPERIENCE: CORPORATE GUILT

In a boat carrying passengers from one part of Alexandria to another, an Italian was spilling cigar ash over an Egyptian woman and her baby, and flapping his newspaper in their faces. When he left his seat to get a drink, two other passengers apologized to the woman. "Thank you," she said, "but why should *you* apologize for him?" "We also are from Italy," they said.

A South American newspaper recently carried a report of a boy of 14 committing a murder, together with the comment of a priest. The priest had said, "When you know the conditions of poverty, over-crowding and disease in which that boy has had to live, you will say that this is our crime rather than his. We, the public, have permitted those conditions to exist."

During the second World War Dr Klara Schlink and a friend were the leaders of a group of 150 Christian women and girls in Darmstadt in Germany. The aim of this group was to help anyone in great trouble. On 11 September, 1944, the town was bombed and completely destroyed by fire, and many people were killed. When those members of the group who had survived met again, they felt more strongly than ever that they must make the best use of their lives. Above all they wanted to make amends because their nation, led by Hitler, had ill-treated the Jews and had murdered more than six million of them while the Nazis were in power. They felt that they shared in the guilt of their nation.

From these three examples, we can see what is meant by the "experience of corporate guilt". We see that it is good that people can share the guilt of their nation. But we have now to ask, "What do people do who have this experience?"

Of the many different ways in which they behave we may note the following:

1. They work hard to make amends for the wrong that has been done. The group which Dr Schlink led in Germany became the Sisters

of Mary, an ecumenical community. One of their activities is to have a house in Israel where they care for Jews who are old and ill.

2. They try to forget it by finding some other group of people whom they can blame for the wrong-doing, e.g. they blame "the Communists" or "the Jews" or "the Whites" or "the Blacks" or "the landlords".

3. They endure the feeling of guilt and know no way of dealing with it. This is such a common experience that two examples of it will be enough.

In most countries of the world there is a wide gap between the prosperous and the very poor. It is often the young people who are especially aware of this gap. They rightly draw other people's attention to it, so that many prosperous people feel guilty about it (though they may not express this feeling). But there is usually no easy solution, for the gap would not be closed even if the prosperous gave most of their property to the very poor. The young people, having (rightly) made the prosperous feel guilty, usually cannot tell them what to do with their guilt.

During the civil war in Zaire, a young army officer belonged to a unit which was ordered to kill large numbers of prisoners, men, women, and children, who had been captured in the war. He and the other members of his unit did this by lining them up six at a time and shooting them with a machine gun. Although he was one of several officers who had had orders from their superiors to do this, he and one other officer were overcome by guilt. They felt so guilty that they made plans to kill themselves. As far as they could see, there was no other way of dealing with their guilt.

When we study Psalm 130 we see from v. 4 that the worshippers had had some experience of this sort. Possibly the Israelites had committed some terrible cruelty upon a neighbouring tribe. Or perhaps they had left the worship of God to join in the worship of some spirit of the soil (a fertility spirit). Whatever had occurred, the worshippers carried the burden of guilt. And from vv. 7 and 8 it seems that the whole nation had been involved: "O Israel".

But the reason why we still turn to Psalm 130 today is that the worshippers were able to see beyond their guilt to God who offered to forgive them.

## 2. THE RECOGNITION OF GOD

(a) The worshippers saw that God was willing to take the first step to restore the relationship between them and Himself. "There is forgiveness *with thee*" (v. 4). The reason why so many guilty people are without hope is that they know that they themselves cannot put things right, and do not know that God does do this.

(b) They saw that God had "steadfast love" (v. 7). We have already noted the Hebrew word *chesed* which is translated "steadfast love" or

157

"loving kindness" or "mercy". See note on p. 37. God promised, as part of the Covenant which he had with His people, that He would treat them with *chesed*. Because they could rely on His *chesed*, there were other truths about God which they saw:

1. God does not punish people according to the number of their sins. He is not like a shopkeeper who keeps an account of each article which a customer has taken. "If thou . . . shouldest keep account of sins who could hold up his head" (v. 3 NEB).

2. God "forgives" guilty people (see v. 4). This means that God takes away whatever barrier there is between them and Himself. The Hebrew word *salach*, here translated "forgive", probably means "remove". See note on p. 65.

3. God "redeems" guilty people (see v. 8), i.e. He rescues them at a cost to Himself. See note on p. 162.

### 3. RESPONSE

The worshippers responded to God who is "steadfast love" with this psalm of hope. They felt like a night-watchman waiting for the morning light to come. There was once a school night-watchman who heard thieves in the night and was so frightened that he locked himself into a classroom all night. He was still asleep when the girls arrived in the morning! A good watchman, on the other hand, stays awake and watches patiently all night, confident that the morning light will come. So the worshippers were confident that God would come, bringing His forgiveness.

Psalm 130 is in two parts:

**Vv. 1–4:** A prayer offered by the leader of the worship: "Lord, listen to us and give us your forgiveness." Perhaps the worshippers asked God to listen because they were not certain that He loved them enough to listen without being asked. Since the coming of Jesus, Christians have believed that God offers them forgiveness even before they have asked for it.

**Vv. 5–8:** The proclamation made by the leader to the congregation: "We are waiting and we are hoping in God" (vv. 5, 6). "We have hope because of what we know about God" (vv. 7, 8).

Verses 5–8 of Psalm 130 are like the chorus of Psalm 62. The plan of Psalm 62 is:

Vv. 1, 2:  Chorus—"For God alone my soul waits in silence."
Vv. 3, 4:  I am being attacked by my friends.
Vv. 5–7:  Chorus (enlarged).
Vv. 8–12:  Let others learn this lesson about God.

### USE

1. It may be that at first this psalm was the prayer of some person or small group of people greatly troubled by their feelings of guilt.

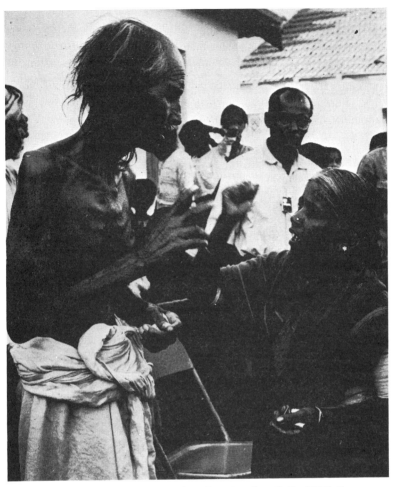

"O Israel, hope in the Lord . . . He will redeem Israel . . ." (Ps. 130.7, 8).

A woman member of a village council in South India tries to persuade an old man to accept the treatment that will set him free from his illness.

But from vv. 7 and 8 it seems likely that it soon became a prayer for the whole congregation.

2. Christians have used this psalm in public worship on many different occasions, e.g. as a preparation for the service of Holy Communion (see especially vv. 5 and 6) or at a burial.

3. This was the psalm which John Wesley heard in St Paul's Cathedral, London, on 24 May 1738. Later that day he came to a great turning point in his life. He knew that God had saved and accepted him, not because he was a good man or because he had repented, but simply because God loved him. Perhaps the words of this psalm helped him to this knowledge.

## NOTES

**Ps. 130.1: Out of the depths.** The Israelites lived in a climate where there were great changes. For part of the year rivers dried up. Then the snow melted in the mountains and the rain came, and suddenly the little streams became deep rushing torrents. So "deep water" became a picture of something to be feared.

Writers of several psalms speak of "the depths" or "deep waters" when they are thinking of troubles from which they cannot escape, but from which they believe that God can rescue them, e.g. "Save me, O God! for the waters have come up to my neck" (Ps. 69.1).

Guilt is itself "deep water". The writer of this psalm knew his guilt. But many people have buried their feelings of guilt deep in their minds because the feelings were too painful to think about. See note on p. 61.

**Ps. 130.4a: There is forgiveness with thee.**

1. What is the forgiveness of God? What does God do when He forgives guilty people?

Both the writer of this psalm and Christians who use it would agree in saying that God sets guilty people free when He forgives them. He sets them free from the condition of being strangers in His presence. He does this simply because of His love for them and because He wants them to live fully. See note on Ps. 130.8b.

The truth about forgiveness may become clearer if we notice in the light of the teaching of Jesus what God does *not* do when He forgives people:

(a) It is not because people are sorry that God forgives them, nor because they confessed their sinfulness. It is true that they cannot receive God's forgiveness until they are sorry. But God does not wait for their repentance before He forgives them. He forgives people before they have repented. Indeed it is God's loving offer of forgiveness which moves people to repent.

(b) It is not because people are trying to make amends for what they did wrong that God forgives them. But it is true that people who are really sorry for doing wrong will try to make amends.

(c) God does not cancel the suffering which may come to people as the result of their wrong-doing. If a palm-wine tapper gets drunk and is then injured by falling from the tree, God offers him complete forgiveness. But God does not remove the man's injury, nor his pain.

(d) Neither God nor the people whom He forgives forget the wrong that has been done. The saying "to forgive is to forget" is not really true.

(e) God does not take away people's feelings of guilt. These feelings are no longer overwhelming, but they do not disappear.

(f) God does not change guilty people into sinless people. When we sing "O thou that takest away the sins of the world", we really mean that God takes away the barrier which our sins have made.

(g) God does not regard people's wrong-doing as unimportant. So when someone really accepts forgiveness from God he does not say "Since God freely forgives me, I can sin as often as I like." See Rom. 2.4: "Do you think lightly of God's wealth of kindness . . . without recognizing that God's kindness is meant to lead you to a change of heart?" (NEB). See also Romans 6.1.

2. What difference has Jesus made by His teaching to our ideas about God's forgiveness?

First, the new and special teaching of Jesus was that God takes the trouble to search out those who need His forgiveness. "The Son of Man came to *seek* and save the lost" (Luke 19.10).

Secondly, Jesus taught that it is when we forgive other people that we are ready ourselves to receive forgiveness from God. "Forgive us our sins, for we ourselves forgive . . ." (Luke 11.4). If we refuse to forgive other people we are making ourselves less able to receive God's forgiveness.

3. What difference has Jesus made (by His life and death and resurrection) to our being forgiven by God? What did Jesus do which no one had done at the time when the Israelites first used this psalm?

All Christians agree that Jesus made a difference not only by His teaching but by His actions, e.g. "Christ died for our sins" (1 Cor. 15.3). Because of Jesus, God's forgiveness is available to us in a new way. But there are different ways in which Christians explain this:

(a) Some emphasize that Jesus by His actions changed the attitude of God towards human beings, e.g. that by dying Jesus provided a sacrifice which satisfied God.

(b) Others emphasize that Jesus changed the attitude of the Devil, who up to the time of Jesus's death had control over all human beings, e.g. that Jesus by dying paid a ransom to the Devil.

(c) Others emphasize that Jesus' actions changed the attitude of human beings, e.g. that God allowed His own Son Jesus to die in order that we human beings should realize how much He loved us.

**Ps. 130.4b: That thou mayest be feared.** When the worshippers recognized God's love for them they felt awe and reverence and fear. We are reminded of the awe which St Peter felt when he discovered that Jesus was completely trustworthy, "Depart from me, O Lord" (Luke 5.8). The Israelites did not take God's forgiveness for granted: they were surprised each time they remembered it. See note on Psalm 67.7. When worshippers sang about "fearing the Lord", they were thinking about all kinds of reverence, e.g. obeying Him in daily life, and honouring Him in public worship. See, for example, Psalm 111.10.

Psalm 111 is a Hymn in which the writer in vv. 1–9 remembers the great things God has done for His People, and praises Him. Then in v. 10 he says, "Therefore reverence God: this is the way in which you start life as a believer: 'The fear of the Lord is the beginning of wisdom'."

**Ps. 130.8b: He will redeem Israel from all his iniquities.**

**Redeem.** This is a translation of the Hebrew word *padhah* which the Israelites used in situations such as the following:

(a) When a man had been sold into slavery, someone could set him free. He could do this by paying the owners the same amount which they had paid for the slave. This man had "redeemed" the slave from the state of slavery.

(b) When the Israelites realized that God was one who rescued them, they used the word "redeem" because it was a costly thing for God to do.

(c) Most writers who used this word meant that God rescued His people from physical suffering or from human enemies. The writer of Psalm 130.8 was saying something different, namely, that God could set His people free from the spiritual state they were in, i.e. the state of being strangers in His presence. See also the note on p. 19 on the Hebrew word *gaal* which is also translated "redeem".

**All his iniquities.** God forgives us whatever our condition. No doubt some sins are more serious in God's eyes than other sins. But He does not have two lists, one of sins that He forgives, and another of sins which He cannot forgive. He offers complete forgiveness to an unfaithful husband, a girl who cheated in school exams, a politician who encouraged two countries to fight each other so that he could make a profit from selling guns to both sides, a writer who was careless about his punctuation.

It is true that Jesus said that to the extent that a person is unable to see any difference between good and evil, to that extent he cannot receive forgiveness. Jesus called this the sin against the Holy Spirit (see

Mark 3.29). But this only means that such a person is preventing God's forgiveness from reaching him. It does not mean that God holds back His forgiveness.

## STUDY SUGGESTIONS

### WORDS

1. What *five* words in the following list have the same or nearly the same meaning:
   group, individual, corporate, associated, single, personal, social, allied.

### CONTENT

2. For what two reasons did Dr Schlink and her friends (of whom we read on p. 156) become concerned about the welfare of Jewish people?
3. Which two verses in Psalm 130 show that the whole people of Israel were sharing an experience of guilt?
4. What words in Psalm 130 suggest that God does not punish human beings according to the number of their sins?

### BIBLE

5. In what two chief ways are the thoughts of Psalm 130 different from those of Psalm 51?
6. (a) What is the chorus of Psalm 62?
   (b) In what way is it like Psalm 130.5–8?
7. Read the following passages and say in each case what we learn about God's forgiveness:
   (a) Ps. 85.1 and 2   (b) Ps. 86.5–7   (c) Ps. 103.3   (d) Ps. 130.4b
   (e) Dan. 9.9   (f) Eph. 1.5–7   (g) Eph. 4.32
8. On p. 162 it is shown that "redeem" usually means to rescue someone at a cost to oneself.
   (i) Read the following passages and say in each case *from what* God redeemed or rescued His people:
      (a) Deut. 7.8   (b) 2 Sam. 4.9   (c) Job 5.20   (d) Ps. 25.22
      (e) Ps. 49.15   (f) Ps. 130.8
   (ii) In what way is the thought contained in Psalm 130.8 different from the thought in the other passages?
9. Read Luke 15.11–32. In what three ways is the attitude of the father in that parable like the attitude of God towards all guilty people?

### DISCUSSION AND RESEARCH

10. "Hear my voice" (Ps. 130.2).

Some people say that since the coming of Jesus, Christians believe that God hears, and that it shows a lack of trust in Him to *ask* Him to "hear" in public or private prayer.

(a) What is your opinion?

(b) What is the practice of your Church concerning prayers of this kind?

(c) Give examples from actual orders of Service.

11. (a) Read a recent copy of a national newspaper and find, if you can, two items of news for which you think the whole nation feels or should feel guilty.

(b) Give an example from your own experience of belonging to a group which had a feeling of "corporate guilt".

12. It is often said that we have been given the service of Holy Communion "because in it the death of Jesus is shown forth so that we may receive forgiveness".

(a) What is your opinion of this?

(b) To what extent do you find that in practice you come away from a Communion service free from a burden of guilt?

13. "God forgives people before they have repented. Indeed it is God's loving offer of forgiveness which moves people to repent" (p. 160). Do you agree? If you do, give an example from everyday life. If you do not, explain your reasons.

14. There is a story on p. 157 of two soldiers who planned to kill themselves.

(a) Why did they want to kill themselves?

(b) If you had met them and they had told you of their plan, what could you have said to them?

15. "In most countries of the world there is a wide gap between the prosperous people and the very poor" (p. 157).

(a) To what extent does this gap exist in your country?

(b) Who are the most prosperous people?

(c) Where do you find the very poor?

(d) What signs are there, if any, that people feel guilty about this gap?

16. What difference has Jesus made to our receiving forgiveness from God? It is said on p. 161 that most Christians answer this question in one of three ways.

(a) What are these three ways?

(b) What is *your* answer?

17. "This is our crime rather than his" (p. 156).

These were the reported words of a priest when he heard of a boy of 14 committing murder.

(a) What did the priest mean?

(b) What would you reply to someone who said the following:

"The priest's words are dangerous. If people take them seriously then anyone can commit a crime and say that he was not responsible"?

18. What would you say to someone who had read Mark 3.29 and said he has committed the unforgivable sin against the Holy Spirit?

# The Right Hand
# Psalm 139

## THEME

### 1. THE EXPERIENCE: AWARENESS OF SELF

In studying Psalms 72, 96, and 100 we have seen that the Israelites worshipped God out of their experience of "belonging". They worshipped Him because they belonged to the nation, because they belonged to the whole human race, and because they belonged to the worshipping congregation. In order to develop as a person, everyone needs to experience belonging, i.e. to have a relationship with other persons. Many people would say more than this. They would say that a person is only fully a person if he has also a relationship with an unseen Power.

All this is true. And yet each of us is aware of being a person who is different from other people. A 9-year-old schoolboy wrote:

Me, I'm me myself,
No one in this big
World is like me.
I'm different from you

And everyone else . . .
Me, I'm myself,
No one's like me,
And I'm not like anyone.

He did not say that he was isolated from others, only that he was different. He was different from those who were closest to him, his parents, his brothers and sisters, his friends. He was responsible for being himself. His conscience was his and no one else's. This is why the great physicist Albert Einstein wrote, "Never do anything that is against your conscience even if the State demands it of you."

But, although each person is aware of himself, he also knows that he only partly knows himself:

There is a part of himself which he knows and which he lets his friends see;

There is a part which he knows and which he does not let anyone see;

There is a part which he does not know but which his friends do know;

There is another part which neither he nor his friends know, but which God knows.

When someone becomes aware of himself, several things can result. Among these, the following are three: (a) he may exaggerate himself and then we call him self-centred or conceited. Or, (b) if he is afraid of himself, he may hide and suppress himself. Or, (c) he may dedicate this "self" to serve some leader or share in some task.

The writer of Psalm 139 had become aware of his "self", even though he realized that he did not fully know himself. (The words "I", " me", "my" occur very frequently in this psalm.) But he looked beyond his "self" to God, and dedicated that "self" to serve Him.

## 2. THE RECOGNITION OF GOD

There are three truths about God which the writer saw clearly: (1) God knows, (2) God is present, (3) God has a purpose.

1. *God knows* everything about us. See especially Psalm 139.1–6. God knows, better than we do ourselves, our real reasons for what we do. "Thou discernest my thoughts" (v. 2). "Search me, O God, and know my heart" (v. 23). "He knows what we are going to say before we say it" (v. 4). As St John said about Jesus: "He knew what was in man" (John 2.25).

When people realize this truth they may feel disturbed, or they may feel comforted and secure.

(a) They feel disturbed because they cannot hide anything at all from God. "I can't even swallow my spit alone," said Job (7.17–20). "The word of God is living ... discerning the thoughts and intentions... all are open and laid bare" (Heb. 4.12, 13). See note Psalm 139.7a "Whither shall I go . . .?"

(b) They feel secure and safe as sheep feel safe because their shepherd knows them. "I know my own" (John 10.14). See also Jeremiah 12.3. They feel secure because God accepts them fully while knowing all about them: "Whenever our hearts condemn us ... God is greater than our hearts and he knows everything . . . we have confidence" (1 John 3.20, 21).

2. God can *be present anywhere* He wishes at any time. He can be active in any way He chooses. See Psalm 139.7–12 and note on Psalm 139.7b.

Many people believe that there are many "gods" or "spirits", and that each "god" or "spirit" has his own area, and is not present outside that area. This is true of those who reverence the "gods" or "spirits" who, so they believe, control mountains or lakes or rivers. Many stories are told today about these "gods" or "spirits", e.g. of Mount Kenya, or Mount Pago in New Guinea, or Lake Bosomtwe in Ghana, or the River Niger.

But the writer of Psalm 139 recognized that the one true God is present everywhere. "If I dwell in the uttermost parts of the sea, even there thy hand shall lead me" (vv. 9–10). God is actively at work in the lawyer in his Ghanaian office, in the Philippine priest visiting a sick man, and in the air-pilot landing his plane with skill at Karachi.

This truth is like the truth that God knows everything: it comforts people, but it also disturbs them.

It is comforting to know that God searches us out when we are in trouble. Jesus said, "What man . . . having a hundred sheep, if he has lost one of them, does not . . . go after the one which is lost . . .?" (Luke 15.4).

But it is disturbing because it may change the way we live. Over the door of the room where the great botanist Linnaeus used to lecture to his students, he had this sentence written: "Live uprightly; God is here."

3. God *has a purpose* and a plan for everything that He has created. See Psalm 139.13–18 and note on Psalm 139.16.

The reason why God knows about us (vv. 1–6) and is present and active among us (vv. 7–12) is that He created us. As the writer of Psalm 139 thought of God as his Creator, he realized that God had a purpose for all that He had created, just as a carpenter has a purpose for the table he has made. See notes on Psalm 139.7a and 16.

The writer of Psalm 139 believed also that God had a plan for himself in particular, even when he was in his mother's womb. "Thou didst knit me together in my mother's womb" (v. 13); and before that: "I was being made in secret, intricately wrought in the depths of the earth" (v. 15).

It affects the way we live if we believe that God has a purpose for us. Jeremiah believed it: "The word of the Lord came to me saying 'Before I formed you in the womb, I knew you'" (Jer. 1.5). St Paul believed it: "We are God's handiwork, created . . . to devote ourselves to the good deeds for which God has designed us" (Eph. 2.10). Jeremiah and St Paul felt that this was a powerful reason for them to devote their lives to God's service.

It may seem to us that we are not free if God has already made a plan for our lives. But this is not so. God *knows* what we shall do. God *guides* our lives and the events of the world according to the plan He has made. God *allows* us to do wrong if we choose to do so. God *controls* all that takes place. But He never chooses some people to be wrong-doers: He leaves us all free. So St Paul said, "Look at your own salvation . . . for God is at work in you" (Phil. 2.12, 13).

3. THE RESPONSE

The response, which is Psalm 139, is a prayer. The worshippers did not sing *about* God: they sang *to* Him. There are two parts:

"O Lord, thou hast searched me and known me!" (Ps. 139.1).

God knows more about this Tahitian girl than she can ever discover about herself.

**Vv. 1–18:** Lord, you know me (vv. 1–6), you are present with me (vv. 7–12), you have a plan for my life (vv. 13–18).

**Vv. 19–24:** Lord, I dedicate myself to fight against evil in your name, and entrust myself to your greater knowledge (v. 23), and to your greater power (v. 24).

So in the second part the writer, who was aware of his "self", dedicated this "self" to the service of God. We remember the words of St Teresa of Avila, the Spanish nun who lived in the sixteenth century:

> I am yours, I was born for You,
> What is Your will for me?
> Let me be rich or beggared,
> Exulting or lamenting,
> Comforted or lonely! . . .
> Since I am Yours, Yours only,
> What is Your will for me?

## USE

1. Perhaps when it was first used, Psalm 139 was the prayer of an Israelite king, who dedicated his authority to God's service and asked for God's help against enemies.

2. It is difficult to know how best to use it in public today. The important part of it is the self-dedication of the worshippers (vv. 19–24). Yet these are the verses which contain the words "Slay the wicked" (v. 19), and which are not usually suitable for public worship. See note on Psalm 139.19.

## NOTES

**Ps. 139.1: Thou hast known me.** When writers of the Bible said that God "knew" people (Hebrew: *yada*), the word had various meanings:

(a) God is aware of events on earth. "I have told the glad news, as thou knowest, Lord" (Ps. 40.9).

(b) God is caring for someone and helping him. "The Lord pities those who fear him. For he knows our frame." (Ps. 103.13, 14.)

(c) God has chosen someone for a special purpose. "You only have I known of all the families of the earth" (Amos 3.2). The word is used in this way in Psalm 139 vv. 1–6.

**Ps. 139.7a: Whither shall I go from thy Spirit?** The writer recognized not only that God cared for him but also that God was his "Lord", i.e. that God had claims upon him. So it was natural that he should want to run away.

It is disturbing to know that God pursues us. We hate His chasing us. We wish He would leave us alone. Francis Thompson was an English poet who experienced God pursuing him. His parents were

Christian and he himself began to train as a priest. But he lost interest. Later he trained as a doctor, but gave up his studies. Then he began to take powerful drugs and lived the life of a beggar in London. Then a woman writer and her husband met him and took care of him in their home. It was then that he recognized God working in those who were caring for him. He realized that he could no longer escape God's love, although it meant that he had to change his way of life. Later he wrote the poem called *The Hound of Heaven*, which begins: "I fled Him down the nights and down the days".

If we have never felt that we wanted to escape from God then it is likely that the god we serve is not the true God, but a god which we have invented. Human beings who face the true God find many ways of trying to escape from Him, e.g.:

They believe that the presence of God is limited to a few special places, e.g. to a church building or to one special form of worship, and in these ways they avoid facing God in other places.

When scholars were making the new translation of the Bible into modern everyday Arabic, an Arab Christian in Jerusalem complained that they were "interfering with the Word of God". One of the scholars said, "No. What we are trying to do is to let the living Word of God reach readers today in their own language. But unfortunately some people treasure the old 'classical' translation so much that they are escaping God Himself." They concern themselves so much with what God has done in the past, or what they hope He will do in the future, that they avoid recognizing God's claim upon them in the present.

**Ps. 139.7b: Thy presence.** The Hebrew word which is here translated "presence" is *panim*. It is sometimes translated "face", "sight", etc.

This word comes from another Hebrew word which means "turning to meet another person and recognizing him". But *panim* usually means "person" or "self", and the AV translation of the word as used in Job. 13.8 is "person".

When writers used *panim* about God, they had in mind the following thoughts:

1. That God is personal. We cannot call Him "a person". If we call Him "a person" we shall begin to regard Him as less than He is. We shall be making God in the image of man. But if we think of him as less than personal, e.g. if we think of Him only as a "force", like electricity, we shall be regarding Him as less than man.

2. That God made Himself known to Moses in a special way on Mt Sinai, when He made the Covenant with the Israelites.

3. That God was present in a special way each time that worshippers met as a congregation in the Temple, and saw the Ark of the Covenant. See General Note A, p. 48, and note on Psalm 42.2.

4. That when God was present, He was present to protect and rescue

His People with whom He had made the Covenant. "May God make His face (*panim*) to shine upon us, that thy . . . saving power may be known" (Ps. 67.1, 2).

**Ps. 139.8: If I make my bed in Sheol, thou art there.** *Sheol* is the word used for the place (or condition) to which people go after death. Most writers in the Old Testament thought that human beings ceased to be in touch with God after death. "I am like the slain that lie in the grave . . . whom thou dost remember no more" (Ps. 88.5). They thought of Sheol as being dark and gloomy. But it may be that this psalm was written after most of the other psalms. Perhaps the writer held different beliefs from earlier writers, and believed that God makes himself known to those who have died. See notes on Psalms 23.6b and 103.16.

**Ps. 139.16: In thy book were written . . . the days that were formed for me.** At first sight it seems that the writer believed that fate controlled his life. It is as if God had a book in which He wrote the story of people's lives before they were born, so that in their lives they were never free.

There have always been people who did think this, and probably some Israelites thought it. Today millions think that if they are born under one special star or planet, that star or planet will control their lives. They believe that there is nothing that they can do to make things better in the world: all they can do is to find out what is going to happen.

Two Hindus in South India who belong to the group called "Saivists" told a Christian how important astrologers were to them. One said, "My astrologer has told me that my business will not be successful until I am forty, so there is no point in my working hard as yet." The other said, "My experience of God is this: when my astrologer warns me that the stars are predicting disaster, then I ask God to prevent or lessen that disaster."

But the writer of Psalm 139.16 did not believe that fate controlled him. He used the phrase God's "book" to mean the purpose or plan which God has for each person.

A Muslim who was born in the oil-fields area of Khuzistan in Iran became a Christian minister in Kerman. He said "From the very early days, when I felt the love of God . . . something untouchable and invisible was always pushing me . . . With all my weaknesses I can simply say that the same Power which called St Paul . . . has called me to carry His Name before these people." See note on Psalm 139.7a. When someone believes this he feels safe and secure. But he also knows that he is free to make his own choices. He knows that God expects him to work for the good of mankind and to overcome what is evil.

**Ps. 139.19: Slay the wicked, O God.** See note on Psalm. 63.9, 10: "Those who seek to destroy my life . . . shall be given over to the power of the

171

sword", and on Psalm 91.8 "You shall watch the punishment of the wicked" (NEB).

1. In this verse and the following verses the writer was saying three things:

(a) When people behave wickedly they are dishonouring God who has a good purpose for mankind. Therefore it is right that they should be destroyed (vv. 19, 20).

(b) I dedicate myself to hate such people and to fight them (vv. 21, 22).

(c) My hating and fighting is not against my own personal enemies (e.g. neighbours who have stolen my cattle), but against God's enemies.

2. Much of this is true, as we have already seen. When the writer became aware of himself, he offered himself to serve God. Serving God meant fighting evil wherever he saw it.

3. But we should notice two truths about God which the writer did not understand:

(a) That God is in control. God is able to contain the evil that is in the world. He does not cease to be God because there is much evil. We should certainly fight evil, but we fight under God's leadership, not in place of God.

(b) That God has compassion on those who do wrong. See note 4 on Psalm 63.9.

**Ps. 139.24: Wicked way . . . way everlasting.** This is a picture of a road which branches to the right and to the left, and the traveller has to choose which way to take. Writers in the Bible and especially in the Psalms often use this picture-language. "The way of the righteous . . . the way of the wicked" (Ps. 1.6). "The way is easy that leads to destruction . . . the way is hard that leads to life" (Matt. 7.13, 14).

In this verse the Hebrew word translated "wicked" really means "which produces pain".

Two other psalms in which the writers compare the "two ways" are 112 and 146.

Psalm 112 is a "Wisdom Psalm" (see note on Ps. 19.7) as well as being a song of praise. Its plan is:

V. 1a: Praise to God.

Vv. 1b–9: A description of a "blessed" man.

V. 10: A "wicked" man.

Psalm 146 also combines instruction with praise:

Vv. 1, 2: Praise to God.

Vv. 3–5: A "happy" man is one who puts his trust in God. (The Hebrew word for "happy" is the same word as that which is translated "blessed" in Psalm 112.)

Vv. 6–9a: Praise to God.

V. 9b: The wicked man.

V. 10: Praise to God.

## STUDY SUGGESTIONS

### WORDS

1. How many times do the words "I", "me", "my" occur in Psalm 139?
2. "Each of us is aware of being a person who is different from other people" (p. 165).
   Which four of the following words have the same or nearly the same meaning as "different" in that sentence?
   opposite   unique   unfriendly   distinct   individual   unpopular   special
3. What is the meaning of *Sheol*?

### CONTENT

4. What three great truths about God does Psalm 139 point to?
5. In Psalm 139 did the worshippers sing *to* God or *about* God?
6. In which verses did the writer of Psalm 139 dedicate himself to the service of God?
7. "Slay the wicked, O God" (Ps. 139.19). What truth did the writer of those words *not* understand?

### BIBLE

8. In what way are the ideas of Psalm 139.8b different from the ideas found in Psalm 6.5 and Psalm 88.5?
9. The Hebrew word *panim* (Ps. 139.7) is usually translated "face" or "presence". How is it translated in each of the following passages:
   (i) In the RSV?
   (ii) In the AV or another English version or in another language?
   (a) Ex. 33.12   (b) Ex. 33.14   (c) Ex. 33.20   (d) Job 13.8   (e) Ps. 19.14   (f) Ps. 27.8   (g) Ps. 42.5b   (h) Ps. 97.5   (i) Ps. 139.7   (j) Ps. 143.2
10. Read the following passages and say in each case:
    (i) Who was escaping or trying to escape from God?
    (ii) Why did he want to escape?
    (iii) What did he do in his efforts to escape?
    (iv) What was the result in the end?
    (a) Gen. 28.10—16   (b) 1 Kings 19.1–18   (c) Jonah 1—4
11. "When writers said that God "knew" people, the word had various meanings" (p. 169), e.g.:
    (i) God is aware of events on earth.
    (ii) God cares for someone and helps him.
    (iii) God has chosen someone for a special purpose.
    Which of these three meanings has the word "know" in each of the following passages?

(a) Ps. 139.1, 2  (b) Jer. 1.5  (c) Nahum 1.7  (d) John 10.14
(e) 1 Cor. 3.20  (f) Gal. 4.7–9

12. (a) Is Psalm 139 a suitable psalm for public worship?
(b) If so, how should it be used?
Give reasons for your answers.

## DISCUSSION AND RESEARCH

13. "If we call God 'a person' we shall begin to regard Him as less
than He is. We shall be making God in the image of man" (p. 170).
(a) Give two examples of words or phrases used in Psalm 139 or in
this chapter which might cause readers to "make God in the
image of man".
(b) Is it possible to do without such words or phrases? If so, suggest
other words or phrases. If not, how can we prevent such words
from leading readers astray?

14. "Lord, thou hast searched me out and known me" (Ps. 139.1).
Read the following passages and say in what way each is (i) like
(ii) unlike Psalm 139.1–6:
(a) Job 7.17–20  (b) Jer. 12.3  (c) Heb. 4.12, 13  (d) 1 John 3.19–21

15. It has been said that a friend is "a person who knows all about
you and loves you in spite of it". What is your opinion? How far
is this a complete description of a "friend"?

16. "Each of us is aware of being a person who is different from other
people" (p. 165).
(a) Is this the experience of everyone? Give examples from everyday
life to illustrate your answer.
(b) Compare the attitude of the boy whose poem is on p. 165 with
that of St Teresa whose poem is on p. 169.

17. "Human beings who face the true God find many ways of escaping
from Him" (p. 170).
(a) Why do people want to escape from God?
(b) Give two examples of ways in which people try to escape God
in addition to those given on p. 170.


# General Note C
# The Psalms were written and collected
## over many years

The Israelites used psalms in their worship of God for at least a
thousand years before the coming of Christ, and hundreds of these
psalms were written down. Then, at some time, one hundred and fifty

of them were chosen and made into one book, which is the Book of Psalms in our Bible. All this we know. But no one knows exactly when each psalm was first used, or how the Book of Psalms was written. We can only say that it probably happened in some way such as this:

1. First, at some time between 1000 BC and 900 BC, someone collected together some psalms which had been used before that time. These are the psalms which are numbered Psalms 3–41 in the Bible. This collection was made in the district round Jerusalem and probably included psalms which David himself had written.

2. A second collection was made about 300 years later, in about the year 650 BC. In the Bible these collected psalms are numbered 42–89. We can now see that they are different from most other psalms because the writers do not use the Hebrew name for God, *Yahweh*, but instead use the name *Elohim*. Probably the person (or group of people) who made this collection used *Elohim* because the name *Yahweh* seemed to him to be too "holy" to use.

This person probably used other smaller collections which had already been made:

(a) The "Songs of the Sons of Korah". Korah was the leader of a choir at Jerusalem and had collected together Psalms 42–49.

(b) The "Songs of Asaph". Asaph led a choir, probably at Bethel, and had collected Psalm 50 and Psalms 73–82.

(c) Some psalms which the priests brought to Jerusalem from the Northern Kingdom after Samaria had been destroyed in 722 BC.

3. A third collection was made in about 460 BC, that is, after the Jews had come back from the Exile. These were psalms which were especially used at religious festivals. This collection contained the following:

(a) "Hallel Psalms" or Praise Psalms (113–118), which were used at the Festivals of Passover, Pentecost, and Tabernacles.

(b) Psalms of "Ascent" (120–134), used *before* festivals, and especially before Passover.

(c) "Hallelujah (Alleluia) Psalms" or Praise-God Psalms (145–50).

4. Finally a group of priests made these three collections into one. They also put a note or "title" at the top of many of the psalms. According to these "titles", seventy-one psalms were "Of David". Others were called "Of Moses", "Of Solomon", "Of Ethan", "Of Asaph", "Of the Sons of Korah". When they called some of the psalms "Of David" they probably meant that these psalms had been written for the kings of the family (or "house") of David. But much later, people believed that David himself had written all the psalms, and at the time when Jesus was teaching this belief was accepted by everyone.

Thus the Psalms were being written and collected over a period of about 800 years.

The above notes are only suggestions, and we must admit that we know only a little about the way in which the Book of Psalms was made. But in spite of this, we can interpret and enjoy and use the psalms to the glory of God.

---

# Bibliography

In addition to the sections on the Psalms in such basic reference tools as *The Abingdon Bible Commentary* and *Peake's Commentary on the Bible*, readers may find the following books useful for further study:

INTRODUCTORY BOOKS
*Psalms*, J. H. Eaton, SCM Press, London
*Reflections on the Psalms*, C. S. Lewis, Bles, London
*God in Man's Experience*, Leonard Griffith, Hodder and Stoughton, London
*Psalms*, A. B. Rhodes, Layman's Bible Commentaries, SCM Press, London
*The Psalms as Christian Praise*, R. B. Y. Scott, Lutterworth, London
*The Psalms for Reading and Recitation*, Alan Neame, Darton, Longman and Todd, London
*Fifty Psalms*, Huub Oosterhuis and others, Burns and Oates Limited, London

MORE ADVANCED BOOKS
*The Psalms*, Artur Weiser, SCM Press, London
*The Faith of the Psalmists*, Helmer Ringgren, SCM Press, London

# Psalms for particular Subjects and Occasions

Those Psalms which are most used in public worship (whether in whole or in part) are given in bold figures.

Advent (see also Kingship, Justice): **19.7–11; 67; 96; 119.129–136; 126**
Ascension: **8; 15; 24; 47;** 21.1–7; 110
Bible: 19.7–14; 119.105–112
Call to worship: **95; 96; 98; 100;** 113; 134
Christmas: **8; 24; 85.8–13; 98; 116.12–19;** 66.1–7
Congregational life (see also Mission): 24; 42; 43; 84; **96; 100;** 122; 147.1–6; 48; 87; 99; 113; 132
Creative work of God: **8; 19.1–6; 29;** 33.1–9; 65; 67; **89.1–18;** 104; 148; 135.1–7
Death, Burial: **23;** 31.21–27; **42.1–7;** 90; 103; 130; 139.1–18
Discipleship, Personal dedication: **1; 15; 19.7–14; 24.1–6; 32;** 112; 119 (espec. 1–16; 33–40; 73–96; 105–112; 129–144; 169–176); 139.1–18; 146; 37; 41; 49; 50; 73; 101; 127; 128; 133
Easter: **16.5–11; 93; 96; 98; 111; 118.14–26; 145.1–7; 146;** 30.1–6; 68.1–8; 113; 114
Epiphany (see also Mission): **36.5–9; 67;** 72.1–11; 89.19–29; 138; **145.1–13**
Evening: 4; 31.1–5; 91; 134
Faith, Trust in God: **4; 16; 23; 27.1–6; 31.21–24; 36.5–9; 46; 63.1–8; 90; 91; 121; 131; 138;** 3; 5.1–8 & 11–12; 11.1–4; 39; 62; 86; 125; 127
Good Friday: **22; 130**
Harvest: **65; 67; 85;** 104.20–29
Kingship and Justice of God: **24; 47; 67; 93; 95; 97.1–9; 98; 99; 100; 145;** 50.1–15; 82
Lordship of God over history: **33; 111; 114; 126; 145;** 76.1–9; 78.1–7; 105.1–15 & 43–45; 106.1–8 & 43–48; 125; 149.1–5

Marriage, Family: **23; 67; 121; 128;** 37.3–7; 127
Mission, Witness: **24; 46; 67; 96; 97; 98; 100; 150;** 87; 117
Morning: **95; 100; 118.19–29**
National life, Leaders: **2; 67; 72; 85; 144.9–15; 146;** 20; 21.1–7 & 13; 45; 61
Peace of the world: **29; 46; 67; 72.1–7; 85.8–13; 96**
Pentecost: **29; 36.5–10; 104;** 25.1–10; 68.1–20
Praise to God: **33; 47; 96; 97; 98; 99; 100; 136.1–9 & 23–26; 146; 147; 148; 150;** 57.7–11; 115; 117; 135.1–7 & 13–21; 149
Presence of God: **16; 23; 63.1–8; 139.1–18**
Redeeming work of God: **34; 36; 85; 103; 116; 130; 136.1–9 & 23–26; 145; 147.1–6;** 78.1–7; 81; 102.12–17; 107; 113
Repentance, Confession: **25.1–13; 32; 51.1–17; 79.8–10; 130;** 6; 14; 38; 41.4–13; 102; 143.1–10
Thanksgiving: **22.23–32; 31.19–24; 32; 34; 40.1–10; 57; 66; 67; 116.1–16; 118.1–19; 136.1–9 & 23–26; 145.1–8;** 18.1–30; 30; 41; 75; 92; 107; 124; 138
Times of trouble: **5; 9.1–10; 16; 22; 27.7–14; 31.1–13; 36; 40.11–17; 41; 42; 43; 57; 63.1–8; 85; 86.1–12; 142; 143;** 6; 7; 10.1–11 & 17–18; 12; 13; 14; 17; 25.1–13; 26; 28.1–2; 6–9; 41; 44.1–8; 52; 53; 54; 55.1–8 & 16–22; 56; 60; 64; 68; 69.1–14; 70; 71; 73; 74; 75.1–7; 77; 79; 80; 83; 88; 89.38–52; 94.1–3 & 16–23; 102; 108; 120; 123; 137.1–6; 140.1–5 & 12–13; 141.1–4 & 8–10
Unity, Fellowship: **15; 97; 122;** 133
Whitsun (see Pentecost)

Note: Psalms 35, 58, 59, 109, 129, have been omitted from these lists because they are generally unsuitable in public worship.

# Key to Study Suggestions

## INTRODUCTION: EXAMPLE, PSALM 118

1. (a) P. 1, lines 10–end.  (b) P. 2, lines 7–15.
2. (a) P. 3, line 1.        (b) P. 2, lines 17–33.
3. (a), (b) P. 1, lines 18–end.  4. (a), (b) P. 7, lines 6–12.  5. P. 5, lines 8–16.
6. They refer to the procession passing through the door of the Temple.
7. Vv. 1 and 29.  8. (a), (b), (c), (d) P. 7, lines 21–end.  9. See pp. 3–6.

## THE CROWN: PSALM 8

1. (b) See p. 13, lines 19–30.
2. (a) (i) and (iii).       (b) See p. 13, lines 4–12.
3. (a) P. 11, line 30.  (b) P. 14, Note 2.
4. P. 10, lines 11–18.  5. P. 14, Note 1.
6. (a) (i) God is Creator, (ii) God is Sustainer, (iii) God is Delegator. (b) (i) 2b or
   3 or 5a, (ii) 4 or 5b, (iii) 5 and 6.
7. There is far more to honour in God than in any human achievement. Therefore
   give Him the honour.
8. (a) Man feels weak in the presence of God.  (b) I will praise God.
   (c) We can see God's glory by looking at the sky.
   (d) God is Saviour, so I shall not be afraid.  (e) I praise God.
9. (a) See 3b, 4, 10–16, 20, 21, 27–32.  (b) See Ps. 145.15, 16.
12. See note on v. 4a, p. 13.

## SWEETER THAN HONEY: PSALM 19

1. Muddle, chaos, disharmony, confusion, irregularity, luck.
2. (a) Conceit, vanity, boasting, obstinacy.
   (b) Courage, confidence, boldness, independence.
3. (a) Judgement, (b) ordinances, (c), what is right, (d) justice, (e) my right, (f) your
   right, (g) justice, (h) judgements, (i) justice, (j) ordinances.
4. Law, testimony, precepts, commandment, fear, ordinances.
5. P. 18, lines 22–32.  6. (a), P. 18, lines 30–32.
7. P. 21, line 5.  8. P. 21, lines 24–29.  9. P. 24, lines 3–14.
10. (a) P. 18, line 25.  (b) P. 18, lines 17, 18.  (c) & (d) P. 18, line 25.  (e) P. 18,
    lines 12–16.  (f) P. 18, lines 29–34.
11. (i) (a).  (ii) (a).  (iii) (a).  (iv) (b).  (v) (b).  (vi) (a).  (vii) (a).  (viii) (b).
    (ix) (b).
12. (1) God is Creator.  (2) God is Creator of order.  See Ps. 148.6.
13. (a) See p. 23, lines 32–34, and p. 24, lines 1, 2.
    (b) Ps. 19.7–10. Both passages use several different words to describe God's
    "law".
15. See note on Ps. 19.11.

## THE MOUTH OF THE LION: PSALM 22

1. (a) Desolation, misery, agony, suffering.  (b) pain, affliction, etc.
2. P. 29, lines 9, 10.  3. P. 29, lines 6, 7.  4. P. 30, lines 1–5.
5. (i) Mark 15.34–37.
   (ii) (a) See Matt. 21.14–17, (b) Luke 23.44–46, (c) John 13.12–21.
6. (1) It is a cry for help.  (2) It gives thanks to God for help given.
7. (1) (a) Experience of being forsaken by God.  (b) v. 1.
   (2) (a) Being mocked.  (b) vv. 7, 8.
   (3) (a) Great thirst.  (b) v. 15.
   (4) (a) Being deprived of his clothes.  (b) v. 18.
   (5) (a) His feet pierced.  (b) v. 16.
8. (a) P. 30, lines 21–24.  (b) P. 32, lines 6–8.  (c) P. 32, lines 3–5.
9. Vv. 1–21. See p. 30, lines 28–30.

# KEY TO STUDY SUGGESTIONS

10. Ps. 99: see p. 29, lines 25–27.  Isa. 8: see p. 29, line 19.
    Hos. 11: see p. 29, lines 28–32.
11. (a) E.g.: enthroned (v. 3), worm (v. 16), bulls (v. 12), lion (v. 13), water (v. 14), wax (v. 14), etc.

## THE SHEPHERD: PSALM 23

1. Reliance on, trust in, faith in.  2. (a) P. 37, lines 18–21.
3. (a) No. See p. 41, lines 40–42.  (b) Yes. See p. 42, lines 33–35.
   (c) No. See p. 42, lines 42–44.
4. (a), (b) P. 40, lines 11–21.  (c) P. 42, lines 11–18.
5. (a) P. 41, last 4 lines. P. 42, lines 1–5.
6. (b) Ps. 51.12, Isa. 40.31, Rom. 12.2.
   (c) Ps. 51.12: restore.  Isa. 40.31: renew.  Rom. 12.2: transform and renewal.
7. (a) V. 6b.  (b) See p. 42, line 31.
9. (a) See p. 40, lines 22–30.

## THE PSALMS WERE FOR TEMPLE WORSHIP: PSALM 24

1. P. 45, lines 3, 4, 15–18, 19–27.  2. (a), (b) P. 46, lines 5–9.
3. (i), (ii) P. 47, lines 27–end.
   (iii) (a) Sacrifice.  (b) Dance or playing instruments.
   (c) Carrying ark or marchings.
   (d) Sacrifice, playing instruments, singing, bowing low.
4. (a), (b) P. 50, lines 11–16.  7. (b) See p. 50, lines 34–39.

## THE FLOWING STREAM: PSALMS 42 AND 43

1. See p. 52, last para.
2. (a) His justice.  (b), (c) The protection He gives.
3. (a), (b) Wait for.  (c), (d), Hope.
4. The writer has courage by trusting or hoping in God.
5. (a) Ps. 27.4b.  (b) Ps. 42.4b & Ps. 43.3b.
   (c) Ps. 84.1a, 2a, 4a, 5, 7b, 10a, 10b.  (d) Ps. 122.1b, 9a.
6. Ps. 4: God of my right; Lord.
   Ps. 43: God in whom I take refuge; God, my God.
7. P. 53, lines 11–16.  8. P. 53, lines 39–43.
9. P. 55, lines 19–23.  10. See p. 51, last para.  14. See p. 58.

## THE OPEN LIPS: PSALM 51

1. Wash, cleanse, teach, purge, fill, hide, create, put, restore, uphold, deliver, open, do, delight.
3. (a), (b), (c) P. 65, lines 21–32.  4. (a), (b), (c) P. 62, lines 24–34.
5. (a) P. 65, lines 33–end.  (b) P. 66, last line.  6. P. 61, lines 20–38.
7. (a) Skill in handwork.  (b) Anger and action.
   (c) New life (breath).  (d) Justice, might.
8. (a) (i) Sinfulness since birth.  (ii) v. 5.
   (b), (c) (i) Repentance.  (ii) v. 3.
   (d) (i) God's gift of a new spirit.  (ii) v. 10.
   (e) (i) P. 66, lines 29–35.  (ii) vv. 16, 17.
   (f) (i) Receiving God's forgiveness.  (ii) vv. 1, 2, 7–12, 14.
9. 2 Sam. 12.12 and Ps. 51.3.
10. The writer of Ps. 38 (1) speaks more about his sufferings and enemies, (2) implies that some of his suffering is undeserved.
16. See p. 161 (second half).

## WATER IN A DRY LAND: PSALM 63

1. Thirsts for, faints for, looked upon, beholding, praise, bless, lift up, call on, think of, meditate on, sing, clings to.
2. (a) P. 70, last para.  (b) P. 71, lines 26–28.
3. P. 70, lines 24–37.  4. P. 71, lines 12–14.

KEY TO STUDY SUGGESTIONS

5. P. 71, lines 18–22.  6. P. 75, lines 27–32.  7. P. 76, lines 3–8.
8. (1) It has in it prayer of longing for God (42.1–4).
   (2) It has prayer of confidence (42.5a).
9. (a), (b) Power to rescue.  (c) Strength or power to create.
   (d) Honour or power.  (e) Strength.  (f) Honour.
10. (a) Pharisees and Herodians.  (b) Friends.  (c) Scribes.
    (d) Judas.  (e) Priests, elders, scribes, guards.
    (f) Pilate.  (g) Samaritans.  (h) Herod and soldiers.
11. (a) He was angry.  (b) He spoke to them.  (c) He went away.
    (d) Drove them out.  (e) He answered them.  (f) Did not resist them.
    (g) Was silent.  (h) Told a parable.  (i) Forgave them.
    (j) Argued with them.
12. (c) Vv. 5–8.  13. (a) V. 5.

THE HARVEST: PSALM 67

1. (a), (b) See p. 85, last para.  (c) Perhaps "judge" and "fear".
2. P. 79, para. 2, and p. 80 top.  3. P. 84, last para.
4. P. 84, lines 41, 42.  5. P. 83, lines 22–26.
6. (a) P. 84, line 1.  (b) P. 83, lines 1–7.
7. (i) (a) God saved them from the Syrians.
       (b) God saved them from the Assyrians.
       (c) God rescued them from Egypt.
       (d) God helped them to cross the Red Sea.
   (ii) (a) Gracious (v. 22).  (b) Saved (v. 22).
       (c) Presence (v. 4).  (d) Saved, mighty power (v. 8).
8. "Steadfast love" (v. 1), "joy" (v. 24), "light" (v. 27).
10. See p. 84, lines 28, 29.  16. (a) Groups.

THE KING: PSALM 72

1. (a) See p. 94, lines 3–9.  (d) P. 94, lines 10–15.
2. P. 89, lines 23, 24.  3. P. 89, lines 1–6.
4. (a) P. 89, lines 13–19.  (b) Saul.
5. (a), (b) P. 91, lines 4–11.
6. (a) P. 93, lines 15–22.  (b) There are many, e.g. v. 13.
7. (a) (ii).  (b) See p. 94, line 23.  (c) (iv).  (d) (iii).  (e) (i) and (ii).  (f) (v).
   (g) (i) and (iii).  (h) (i) and (v).  (i) (i) and (v).
9. (d) See p. 92, note b.  14. See p. 95, lines 6–end.

THE WINGS THAT PROTECT: PSALM 91

1. Deliver, cover, give . . . charge of, guard, bear up, protect, answer, be with,
   rescue, honour, satisfy, show.
2. Snare, terror, arrow, pestilence, destruction, evil, scourge, stone.
3. E.g.: confidence, faith, belief.  4. P. 98, lines 30, 32, 35, 42.
5. (i) Untrue. See p. 101, last para.  (ii) True. See p. 100, lines 2–19.  (iii) True.
   See p. 103, Note on 91.8.
7. Ps. 4: (a) See vv. 1 and 2.  (b) See vv. 3, 7a, 8.
   Ps. 121: (a) See vv. 1b, 3, 7a.  (b) See vv. 2a, 3, 4, 5, 7, 8.
8. (a) P. 101, lines 30–35.  (b) P. 101, lines 36–end.  (c) P. 98, lines 13–17.
9. (a) Angels.  (b) God cares for His people and guides them.

A NEW SONG: PSALM 96

1. Sing, bless, tell, declare, ascribe, bring, come, worship, tremble, say.
2. (a), (b) P. 109, lines 22–29.  3. P. 109, lines 15–17.
4. P. 107, lines 30, 40.  5. (a), (b) P. 113, lines 14–24.
6. (a) A new song.  (b) P. 109, last para.
7. Ps. 47: vv. 5, 7, 8, 9.  Ps. 93: vv. 1, 2.  Ps. 95: vv. 3, 6.  Ps. 97: vv. 1, 9.
   Ps. 98: vv. 6, 9.  Ps. 99: vv. 1, 2.  Ps. 100: vv. 1, 4.
8. (a) (ii).  (b) (i).  (c) (i).  (d) (ii).  (e) (ii).  (f) (ii).  (g) (i).  (h) (i).

9. (a) (iii).   (b) (iii).   (c) (i).   (d) (iii).   (e) (ii).   (f) (i).   (g) (ii).   (h) (i).   (i) (ii).
(j) (iii).

## A PSALM TO BE SUNG: PSALM 98

1. (a) See p. 117, lines 7–23.   (b) P. 117, lines 28, 29.
2. P. 116, last 8 lines.   3. P. 118, lines 8–16.
4. (a) They used the large harp.   (b) Joyfully.   (c) With sacrifices.
5. (b) 46: v. 7.   49: v. 12.   56: v. 4.   62: vv. 1, 2.   67: v. 3:   80: v. 3.   99: v. 5.
107: v. 6 with v. 8.   118: v. 1b.
6. (a) Saying goodbye.   (b) Travelling.   (c) Attacking an enemy.
(d) Welcoming father.   (e) Comforting Saul.   (f) Processing with the ark.
(g) Mourning.   (h) Praising God.
7. P. 126, line 21.

## SHOUTS OF JOY: PSALM 100

1. (a) See v. 3a and p. 131, lines 23–36.
(b) In Ps. 100 the words are followed by reasons for worshipping. See p. 133,
lines 1–4.
2. Loyalty, trustworthiness, reliability, steadiness.
3. (a) Cheerfulness, light-heartedness, merriment, gaiety.
(b) P. 133, lines 17–28.
4. P. 133, lines 6–10.
5. P. 130, last para. and p. 131, lines 1–15.
6. P. 131, lines 2, 3, or p. 134, lines 3–11.
7. (a) They are an invitation to worship.
(b) They give reasons for worship.
8. (a) His steadfast love endures for ever.
9. (a) All human beings.   (b) P. 134, lines 8–11.
10. (a) (i) Seventy.   (ii) The demons were subject to them.
(b) (i) All the disciples.   (ii) They had seen Jesus's mighty works.
(c) (i) The disciples.   (ii) Jesus would see them again.
(d) (i) The disciples.   (ii) They ask and receive.
(e) (i) Peter and apostles.   (ii) They were suffering for Jesus's name.
(f) (i) People of Samaria.   (ii) Many people had been healed.
(g) (i) The Gentiles.   (ii) The word of God was being preached to them.
(h) (i) The jailer and his family.   (ii) He believed in God.
(i) (i) Christians.   (ii) The Spirit is in them.
(j) (i) Those who read the letter.   (ii) They love Jesus and believe in Him.
11. (a) (i), (ii), (iii).   (b) (i).   (c) (iii).   (d) (ii).   (e) (iii).
12. (a) Each verse ends with the Chorus.

## THE EAGLE: PSALM 103

1. Monotony, repetition, routine.   2. P. 138, lines 12–21.
3. (a) P. 138, lines 29–34.   (b) P. 139, lines 14–19.
(c) P. 139, lines 20–22; p. 143, lines 29–40.
4. See p. 138, lines 28–38.   5. They are psalms of praise.
6. (a) P. 144, lines 30–32.   (b) P. 145, lines 14, 15.   (c) P. 145, lines 16–19.
8. See p. 139, lines 6–10.

## THE BROKEN CHAINS: PSALM 116

1. Heard, inclined, saved, dealt bountifully, delivered, loosed.
2. (a) (i) The loyal.   (b) (i) Saints.   (c) (i) Faithful ones.
(d) (i) The godly.   (e) (i) Godly.   (f) (i) Saints.
(g) (i) The faithful.
3. (a) P. 152, lines 30–35.   (b) P. 148, last para.   (c) P. 150, last 2 lines, and p. 151,
lines 1–3.
4. P. 148, lines 8–13.   5. P. 150, lines 6, 7.
6. P. 150, last 2 lines, and p. 151, lines 1–3.

181

# KEY TO STUDY SUGGESTIONS

8. P. 153, lines 33–38.
9. (a), (b), (c) Keeping God's law.  (d) Obeying their own gods.
(e) Being loyal to the true God.

## THE NIGHT-WATCHMAN: PSALM 130

1. Group, corporate, associated, social, allied.
2. P. 156, lines 25–31.  3. P. 157, lines 31, 32.
4. P. 158, lines 5–8.
5. E.g.: Ps. 51 emphasizes the seriousness of sin more than Ps. 130. Ps. 130 emphasizes hope in God.
6. (a) P. 158, line 37.  (b) P. 158, lines 32–35.
7. (a) P. 162, lines 34–41.  (b) P. 160, line 32.  (c) P. 162, lines 34–41.
(d) P. 162, line 8.  (e) P. 160, line 32.  (f) P. 161, line 37.
(g) P. 161, line 27.
8. (i) (a) Egypt.       (b) Early death.   (c) Early death.
(d) All troubles.   (e) Early death.   (f) Spiritual state of sin.
(ii) See p. 162, lines 28–33.
9. E.g.: See p. 160, line 32; p. 161, line 25; p. 162, line 34.
18. See p. 163, lines 1–3.

## THE RIGHT HAND: PSALM 139

1. 48.  2. Unique, distinct, individual, special.
3. P. 171, lines 4, 5.  4. P. 166, lines 13, 14.
5. P. 167, last line.  6. P. 169, lines 3–5.
7. P. 172, lines 14–21.  8. P. 171, lines 4–12.
9. (a) (i) My sight.  (b) (i) Presence.  (c) (i) Face.
(d) (i) Him.  (e) (i) Thy sight.  (f) (i) Face.
(g) (i) My God.  (h) (i) Before.  (i) (i) Presence.
(j) (i) Before.
10. (a) (i) Jacob.  (ii) He had cheated Esau.  (iii) Left his father's house.
(iv) He was reconciled to Esau (Gen. 33.4).
(b) (i) Elijah.  (ii) Jezebel was trying to kill him.  (iii) Went into the wilderness.
(iv) God sent him back to work (1 Kings 19.15).
(c) (i) Jonah.  (ii) He did not want to go to Nineveh.  (iii) Got on a ship going to Tarshish.  (iv) He reached Nineveh and the people repented.
11. (a) (i).  (b) (iii).  (c) (ii).  (d) (ii).  (e) (i).  (f) (ii) and (iii).

# Index

Bold type indicates specially full or important references

## 1. SUBJECT INDEX

183

## 2. PSALMS RECEIVING SPECIAL COMMENT